Alternate
Reality
Games

Gamification for Performance

Alternate Reality Games

Gamification for Performance

Charles Palmer
Harrisburg University of Science and Technology, PA, USA

Andy Petroski
Harrisburg University of Science and Technology, PA, USA

CRC Press
Taylor & Francis Group
Boca Raton London New York

CRC Press is an imprint of the
Taylor & Francis Group, an **informa** business

AN A K PETERS BOOK

CRC Press
Taylor & Francis Group
6000 Broken Sound Parkway NW, Suite 300
Boca Raton, FL 33487-2742

© 2016 by Taylor & Francis Group, LLC
CRC Press is an imprint of Taylor & Francis Group, an Informa business

No claim to original U.S. Government works

Printed on acid-free paper
Version Date: 20151019

International Standard Book Number-13: 978-1-4987-2238-4 (Paperback)

Library of Congress Cataloging-in-Publication Data

Names: Palmer, Charles, author. | Petroski, Andy, author.
Title: Alternate reality games : gamification for performance / Charles
Palmer, Andy Petroski.
Description: Boca Raton : CRC Press, 2016. | Series: An A K Peters book |
Includes bibliographical references and index.
Identifiers: LCCN 2015039394 | ISBN 9781498722384 (alk. paper)
Subjects: LCSH: Vocational education--Computer games. | Vocational
education--Data processing. | Computer games. | Shared virtual
environments.
Classification: LCC LC1048.C57 P35 2016 | DDC 370.1130285--dc23
LC record available at http://lccn.loc.gov/2015039394

Visit the Taylor & Francis Web site at
http://www.taylorandfrancis.com

and the CRC Press Web site at
http://www.crcpress.com

There are many people that have supported our work with Alternate Reality Games and gamification for performance, along with the writing of this book. Thank you to those listed below as well as those who we are ashamedly forgetting to note and the players who are the key to it all!

Drew Davidson

Justin Detig

Janet Dubble

Randall Fujimoto

Harrisburg University of Science & Technology

Koreen Olbrish

Anthony Ortega

Paula Palmer

Madison Palmer

Pennsylvania Educational Technology Conference & Expo

Melissa Peterson

Kelli Petroski

Powerful Learning Practice

Robert Pratten

Lee Sheldon

Jesse Schell

The Deep Sleep Initiative Team

Professor Mary Waller Ph.D

Contents

Preface, ix

CHAPTER 1 WHY AM I NEGOTIATING WITH ALIENS
DURING SALES TRAINING?   1

  THE ARG JOURNEY   2
  ARG EXAMPLES   3
  AN ARG OR NOT AN ARG   6
    An ARG Is *Not* eLearning   6
    An ARG Is *Not* a Computer Game   6
    An ARG Is *Not* Geocaching   7
    An ARG Is *Not* a Scavenger Hunt   7
    An ARG Is *Not* Live Action Role-Playing   8
    An ARG Is *Not Just* Social Learning   8
    An ARG Is *Sort of* Gamification   9
    An ARG Is Transmedia   9
  THE LEARNING CONNECTION   9
  THE BUSINESS APPLICATIONS   12
  ENDNOTES   14

CHAPTER 2 NEW EMPLOYEES SHOULD BE FINDING THE CEO   15
  ARG 1: IMMERSION INTO NEW PROGRAMS   16
  ARG 2: TEAMWORK AND COLLABORATIVE NARRATIVE   19
  ARG 3: OPTIMIZE TRAINING TIME   19
  ARG 4: INCREASED SKILLS   20

FUELING INNOVATION AND OTHER
ORGANIZATIONAL BENEFITS   21
FULL PARTICIPATION   22
MULTIPLE RABBIT HOLES   24
THE BUDDY SYSTEM   24
BAIT-AND-SWITCH   24
ENDNOTES   25

CHAPTER 3 KEEPING UP WITH THE JONESES   27
OTHER ARGS TO EXPLORE   37
ENDNOTES   37

CHAPTER 4 ALL THE WORLD IS A STAGE   39
BUILDING AN ARG   40
INITIATION   41
PREPRODUCTION   42
Build the Teams   42
Define the Goals, Objectives, and a Preliminary Schedule   42
Design the Experience   44
Document the Idea and Development Process   45
Build a Media Plan   46
Put It All Together   46
PRODUCTION   46
Use a Treatment to Prototype the Experience   47
Building the Components   48
Preparing to Fail   48
POSTPRODUCTION   49
GO-LIVE   49
Starting the Game   49
Monitoring the Experience   50
Ending the Game   51
DEBRIEF   51
ENDNOTES   52

Chapter 5 Storytime	53
PLAYER TYPES	55
STORY STRUCTURE	59
CREATING YOUR ARG STORY	60
Start with a Plot, Setting, and Subject	60
Create Characters	62
Consider the Physical Space	64
Consider the Timeline	65
Create the Rabbit Hole	65
Create a Backstory	66
Tell the Story across Multiple Mediums	66
Incorporate Collaborative Storytelling	66
Simple Is Better Than Complex	66
ENDNOTES	67
Chapter 6 10 Participation Points for Gryffindor	69
AVOID TECHNOLOGY DISTRACTIONS	69
MAKE A PLAN	70
EVALUATE PLAYER ACTIVITIES	71
IDENTIFY TECHNOLOGIES BASED ON PARTICIPATION	73
Passive Participation	74
Passive—physical.	74
Passive—digital.	74
Active Participation	75
Active—physical.	75
Active—digital.	75
Immersive Participation	76
Find the Future.	77
The Black Watchmen.	77
CREATING SPECIFIC INTERACTIONS	78
Puzzles	79
Platforms	81

Competition 82
Social Connections 84
ENDNOTES 88

CHAPTER 7 DINOSAUR OR PERFECT BIRD PERCH 89
MOBILE AND WEARABLE DEVICES 93
HEAD-MOUNTED DEVICES 94
GAMIFICATION 95
BLENDED GAMES 97
ARG TECHNOLOGY 98
CONCLUSION 98
ENDNOTES 98

CHAPTER 8 THE SEARCH FOR ONE-EYED WILLY 101
THE BOOK WEBSITE 101
THE BOOK RESOURCES 101
ARG Conferences 102
ARG Game Sites 102
Models 102
Presentations 103
Production Resources and Examples 103
Publications 104
ARG Resource Sites 104

REFERENCES, 105

GLOSSARY, 109

INDEX, 115

Preface

In 2012 Deloitte Consulting identified *gamification* as a business disruptor and one of the Top 10 Technology Trends of the year,[1] predicting that "game mechanics such as leaderboards, achievements, and skill-based learning are becoming embedded in day-to-day business processes, driving adoption, performance, and engagement." Many other industry leaders deemed 2012 "The Year of Gamification."

In 2012, *gamification* was roughly defined as "applying game mechanics and game design techniques in non-game environments to engage and motivate people for behavior change." At the time, the application of gamification was often found in marketing rewards and health management programs but was also gaining traction in enterprise applications like salesforce.com and entertainment websites like the community site for the NBC TV show *The Office*. Since that time, the term *gamification* has been co-opted by everyone with even the simplest game mechanics integrated into their design. This has especially been the case in training and education where multiple-choice quizzes in online learning, once known as knowledge-checks, have been dubbed "gamification" by many. That's the extreme end of the spectrum, but it's an indication of the ubiquitous use of the term *gamification*, ultimately resulting in an overall lack of meaning. You really can't be sure what someone in education or training is referring to when they say "gamification." Even the use of the term to describe employees and students playing *serious games* or simulations to learn and practice new skills is disconnected from the original intent of the word. Gamification is not "playing games." It is embedding game mechanics in some daily activity other than playing a game—such as shopping, exercising, or formatting a spreadsheet—making that experience more enjoyable and more efficient and generally resulting in better outcomes than there would be without the integration of game mechanics.

It's no wonder that education and training professionals have exploited the term. Education and training have long known the benefits of games as highly effective training and learning mechanisms. Serious games or immersive learning environments have been used by the military and Fortune 500 organizations for practicing soft skills, mechanical operations, and sales techniques since the late 1980s. However, it's been difficult for serious games to gain traction in training inside most organizations. The C-Suite (CEOs, CFOs, COOs, etc.) doesn't want their employees "playing games" and they also feel that "learning/work shouldn't be fun." However, the C-Suite is paying attention to gamification. It's predicted that by 2018, the global gamification market will reach $5.5 billion.[2] Enterprise gamification is having an impact on new technology adoption, sales performance, and overall employee satisfaction. And, the C-Suite often sees a direct connection to the bottom line from gamification, more than they can often connect outcomes to training efforts. So, training and education professionals have taken the opportunity to generalize the term *gamification* as a way of gaining acceptance for serious games, simulations, and other immersive learning solutions.

Then, of course, there are training and performance improvement efforts that include a blend of strategies. Immersive learning, blended learning, micro-learning, serious games, simulations, **social learning**, stories, gamification, and a variety of other formats are being used in unique and interesting amalgamations for ongoing, embedded knowledge, and skill development. **Alternate reality games** *(ARGs)* fall into this category, the "other" category. As you'll read in Chapter 1 ARGs are a form of gamification, serious game, simulation, and other familiar experiences with a focus on motivation, **active learning**, and collaboration for improved learning and performance. ARGs are "sort of" gamification. You'll read more about that later.

This book provides the introduction needed to begin strategizing, designing, and developing an ARG for your business or organization. The book focuses on using ARGs for training, but there is also a more general connection made throughout to performance improvement. Training may be a part of performance improvement, but process re-engineering, change management, and innovation efforts are elements of performance improvement that can also benefit from an ARG. However you refer to ARGs—gamification, serious game, simulation, or other—consider an ARG as an organizational tool for improving training outcomes and employee performance. Why? How? Well, read on and find out!

ENDNOTES

[1] Top 10 Technology Trends—http://bit.ly/0_Deloitte
[2] What is Gamification—http://bit.ly/0_Gamification

CHAPTER 1

Why Am I Negotiating with Aliens during Sales Training?

It's late on a dark, warm summer evening in your new city and the first night of your new life. You just attended a welcome reception for new arrivals to the city held by a mayoral candidate looking for support in the upcoming election. You leave the event with a full stomach and an appreciation for the candidate's views, even if he is a politician. You return to your new home ready to put yourself and the first day of your new life to rest. As you walk through the lobby of the building you now call home you notice the candidate's posters on the walls, as you did when you left the building just hours ago. But, there's something different now. As you approach one of the promotional posters you read, "Don't trust him, he's a fraud" on the right side of the poster and see a faint red *X* marked over-top the entire piece. In the bottom left you read, "Big Yellow Taxi." Before leaving the reception you volunteered to help staff the candidate's booth at the upcoming community fair. Now you're reading that he's a fake. Who defaced the posters? Why is the candidate a fraud? What should you do next to explore this mystery?

This scenario could be played out in a book or a movie or an entertainment game, but it could also be part of a corporate training event for new employees or a new student orientation for college freshmen. It is, in fact, the scenario for an alternate reality game (ARG) being created for college freshmen at Harrisburg University of Science & Technology. Businesses and universities are using ARGs for orientation, training, and collaboration exercises. They are using ARGs to take advantage of the story, collaborative **gameplay**, and the combination of physical world and digital experiences as part of learning activities. Players must discover facts, find resources, and collect assets to compete in the game and by doing so they evaluate information and data, connect with new people, and learn new skills. By tapping the benefits of "**hard fun**" in an ARG, players (i.e., employees or students) are engaged and immersed in learning about the latest products, the personnel at the university, or the policies at their new company.

Hard fun describes an experience where the participant enjoys the difficulty inherent in learning a new skill or changing behavior because there is a balance of support, freedom, and challenge in the experience.

THE ARG JOURNEY

An ARG is built around a story that engages the players through an anomaly in their regular daily schedule. It could be an email from an unknown source. It could be a Post-it note on a desk. It could be a video played on a monitor in a public location. Or, it could be a message on a computer screen that reads, "Follow the white rabbit." The realism of the story is strong at the beginning of the ARG. The player might not be sure whether he is even playing a game. The realism may fade as the interaction with content and the level of activities in the game increases, but the story is always there and remains a central part of the player's experience in the game. The ARG experience can take place over a series of days, weeks, or months depending on your goals, audience, and budget.

Most ARGs include a combination of real-world activities in a physical location and digital media. The I Love Trees ARG, created by the Center for Advanced Entertainment and Learning Technologies (CAELT) at Harrisburg University, took place at PETE&C, an educational technology conference held at a convention center in Hershey, Pennsylvania. The Beast, an entertainment ARG created to promote the movie *A.I.*, included anti-robot militia rallies in New York, Chicago, and Los Angeles. The Skeleton Chase ARG took Indiana University freshmen throughout the

Bloomington campus in an effort to increase physical activity and fitness awareness. The Elmwood Park Zoo ARG, created by Melissa Peterson at Oregon State University, engaged visitors at exhibits throughout the zoo.

Social interaction with other players and *non-player characters* in the game can also be a large part of activity in an ARG. The social learning in an ARG can occur face-to-face or through digital and social media tools. The social interaction further enhances the *constructivist* approach to learning inherent in an ARG and takes advantage of the benefits of learning through social media that so many companies are currently trying to tap into.

Non-player characters is a generic term used to describe fictitious people that the player may interact with in the game.

ARG EXAMPLES

ARGs are engaging and motivating. Players discover information and develop new skills through personalized gameplay, versus being passive participants in learning. In an ARG, players learn by doing and discovering while interacting with systems and people that they will ultimately need as resources to succeed in their role as an employee, member, attendee, or student. Skills and knowledge are important, but so are critical thinking, teamwork, and problem solving. ARG experiences allow players to practice those more *tangential skills* as well as gain knowledge and develop job specific skills. Table 1.1 is a list that includes descriptions of some ARGs and information about the sponsors, goals, and learning outcomes.

TABLE 1.1   ARG Examples

ARG	Brief Description	Goals	Outcomes
Que Syrah Syrah[2] Creator: Tandem Learning Sponsor: Constellation Academy of Wine	Learners practiced data analysis, relationship building, and other selling techniques with fictional hotel customers. Players used descriptions of hotel characteristics and information about target customers, menus, wine lists, and sales data as they interacted with customers in various sales scenarios.	Improve the performance of more than 350 field sales managers in selling Constellation brands and positioning those products effectively among competitors	Participation in the game was voluntary, but about 84 percent of the sales force participated in the ARG. Learners thought the game challenges "felt real" and represented exactly what they faced in the field. The sales force asked to continue the training for future learning initiatives.
Find the Future at NYPL: The Game[3] Creators: Jane McGonigal, Kiyash Monsef, and Natron Baxter Sponsor: New York Public Library	Participants assembled at the New York Public Library (NYPL) to create essays about library artifacts, culminating in a printed book focused on "ways to make history and change the future." Players scanned marked artifacts to log them on a game website where players could view presentations of found artifacts and reveal a related essay assignment, focused on how the past and future are intertwined.	Transform a traditionally individual environment and activity into a collaborative one	Five hundred (500) essays were written about one hundred (100) library artifacts, all combined into one book; all done in one evening.
I Love Trees Creator: Center for Advanced Entertainment & Learning Technologies at Harrisburg University Sponsor: PA Educational Technology Expo & Conference (PETE&C), Powerful Learning Practices (PLP)	Participants took on the persona of a new principal at West Side High, whose superintendent has asked for research on Powerful Learning Practices (PLP) and to determine how the techniques can be integrated into the school district. The players were tasked with growing the school's tree of knowledge by advancing their understanding of PLP. Players gathered clues, completed puzzles, networked with vendors, and discovered information to grow the PLP tree of knowledge for West Side High.	Discover Powerful Learning Practices (PLP); reflect on evidences for change in education; redefine teaching practices that take advantage of new tools and technologies that are enabling change; and make connections to impact professional learning.	One hundred and eighty-two (182) conference attendees participated in the game and were introduced to Powerful Learning Practices (PLP). A small focus group confirmed the learning goals were achieved.

Elma Wood's Species Discovery[1] Creator: Melissa Peterson at Oregon State University Sponsor: Elmwood Park Zoo	Zoo visitors interacted with the animal exhibits in new ways. Visitors were asked to help Elma Wood, a zoo biologist, look for new species of animals. Visitors took notes and sketched new species based on observation, creative thinking, and clue-based gameplay throughout multiple exhibits.	Motivate visitors to interact with the animals in the exhibits in new ways to develop a deeper understanding of traits and adaptations. Increase the level of engagement with the exhibits	While exploring the zoo, visitors spent (on average) double the amount of time engaging with the game-flagged exhibits compared to the rest of the exhibits they visited.
Spring Revival[4] Creator: HT2 Sponsor: Warwick Business School Motivate players to learn more about the models and theories that they need to leverage in order to create better businesses	Players accessed a company website, emailed with virtual employee characters, called live telephone lines, and interacted with live actors in the role of employees and leadership to come up with a plan to save a failing water company.	Experiential learning for the induction week of the Postgraduate Diploma in Applied Management at Warwick Business School	HT2 reported increased engagement, collaborative learning, discovery learning, and positive student feedback about the immersion of the gameplay.

AN ARG OR NOT AN ARG

As you can see from Table 1.1, no ARG is like another. Yes, there are common elements in every ARG, but each one really is its own unique design and player experience. Because of their uniqueness, the ARG experience is difficult to briefly describe. It is also difficult to demonstrate an ARG as one might demonstrate interactive multimedia or play a video. Most ARGs happen at a point in time and are from a single, personal, point of view. They are live! So, it's difficult to show an ARG after the fact. The best way to take a deeper dive into defining ARGs is to explore elements of more traditional digital media for training and entertainment and look at how ARGS are different while also borrowing elements from each medium. It's almost easier to describe ARGs by identifying what an ARG is not.

An ARG Is *Not* eLearning

Standard online learning, or **eLearning**, is normally an individual experience that occurs over a short period of time (an hour or two). Most eLearning is content driven with interactions that depend more on mouse clicks than cognitive challenges. The eLearning experience is predefined and there is often little opportunity for adjusting the design or experience based on learner interaction and feedback, until version two.

An ARG normally happens over an extended period of time, from two days to two years (or more), and is interwoven throughout the daily activities of the players. The game is part of life. And, life is part of the game. Gameplay is centered on solving problems or mysteries and identifying hidden opportunities. Technology is often a part of gameplay, but the primary activities are research, collaboration, and problem solving. Depending on how players interact with the game, the **puppet-master** can adjust the game design at any point in the game to make challenges easier or more difficult. The puppet-master manages the resources and game systems from behind the scenes, unbeknownst to the players and sometime removed from the environment. They make adjustments to the ARG story and gameplay when player actions, or inactions, create circumstances that require a change of direction to keep the game on track to achieve its goals.

An ARG Is *Not* a Computer Game

Computer games for learning, or serious games, are created to put concepts in the context of performance and promote behavior change through problem-based learning. However, most serious games are bound to the desktop, the browser, or mobile devices. They are not integrated with the world around you. While serious games can be longer-term experiences, they are normally incremental engagements: for instance, multiple 15- to 30-minute interactions over a period of time.

ARGs are longer-term experiences and are not bound to the desktop, the browser, or mobile devices. ARGs are not computer games, but ARGs for learning can be considered serious games. In addition, an ARG could include a computer game and interaction through the desktop, browser, or mobile devices as part of the ARG experience. And, like a computer game, an ARG involves a story, a goal, and obstacles to achieving the goal. But, beyond the computer, there are also interactions with people, places, or objects in the physical world as part of an ARG experience.

An ARG Is *Not* Geocaching

Geocaching is a recreational activity that challenges participants to find hidden treasures around the world. Participants both hide and seek **geocaches**, which are containers that include an item and a logbook for noting those who find the item, as part of participating in the activity. Communicating the "hide and seek" of caches is based on Global Positioning System (GPS) coordinates that are recorded on a geocache listing site(s).

An ARG may include a challenge that requires players to find items based on GPS coordinates, but an ARG also includes a variety of other challenge activities—anything from talking with other players to gathering information and getting directions to solving puzzles based on available information. And, all of the ARG activities are based around a story and solving a problem or achieving a goal within the context of the story.

An ARG Is *Not* a Scavenger Hunt

We've all participated in a scavenger hunt. In a scavenger hunt, you're provided with a list of items that you must collect during a certain timeframe. Scavenger hunts are mostly recreational and often pit teams of players against each other in a race to find all of the items on the list before the deadline. Some scavenger hunts include clues to finding the items on the list. Often, the clue for finding each item is revealed sequentially. In other words, the clue for item 2 is revealed when item 1 is found.

Many ARGs do follow the structure of a scavenger hunt, but the ARG experience is much deeper than a recreational scavenger hunt. The goal of the ARG is to solve a problem or overcome a business or societal challenge, not just to find all of the items on the list. The ARG is also a mix of real world and computer or virtual experiences. In most cases, scavenger hunts are all about finding and collecting physical items. The story element of an ARG also differentiates the experience from a scavenger hunt. An ARG includes context, characters, antagonists, challenges, decisions, and outcomes that are driven by a story that themes the entire experience.

An ARG Is *Not* Live Action Role-Playing

LARPing or *live action role-playing* is a form of gaming where the players participate in gameplay by physically acting out their characters' actions in the game (often in full costume). The player interacts with other live characters in a scenario that is bound by gameplay rules determined by the players. An ARG may contain live characters, often included as elements of the storyline. But, ARG players do not play as a character in the game. They play the ARG as themselves in their real-life professional or personal role. For example, Principal Wiggins was a character that handed out gameplay material at the educational technology conference for the I Love Trees ARG, briefly described earlier. The Principal Wiggins character was part of the ARG storyline via video, via Tweets, and as a live actor at the event. The ARG players interacted with the Principal Wiggins character, but only as part of gameplay. The players themselves did not play a character role.

An ARG Is *Not Just* Social Learning

The term *social learning* often represents short, digital interactions between individuals to support research, problem solving, content curation, and collaboration that results in learning and performance improvement. Businesses are using discussion forums, employee profiles, search mechanisms, community perception, and crowdsourcing as part of social learning initiatives. The goal is to connect employees for peer learning and learning from subject matter experts in a way that is integrated throughout the workday, versus training as only a single, scheduled event. Online social learning is often an element of an ARG and face-to-face interactions are also a part of the social learning in the game. ARG players not only get updates and participate in gameplay through Tweets, forum posts, and other social learning tools, but they talk, meet, and work together face-to-face to plan gameplay strategy and play the game. The social aspect of ARG gameplay, digital or otherwise, can be primary or complementary in the pursuit of information, skill-building, and critical thinking through other gameplay elements.

An ARG Is *Sort of* Gamification

Gamification is the application of game thinking and **game mechanics** to *nongame* contexts to promote behavior change. It has grown from frequent purchaser clubs and other collection-based marketing programs to include rewards for recycling, making healthy decisions, and effectively managing finances. Also, gamification is often generalized as the rewarding of badges and points in a competitive, nongame environment. Points are also awarded in an ARG and badges can also be incorporated for completing increasingly difficult tasks at various levels. An ARG for business *is* focused on behavior change. But an ARG *is* a game. It is not a traditional game, but it is a game. The players may not know it's a game to begin with or even describe what they are doing as playing a game. Ultimately, ARGs intersect the boundaries between playing a game and performing daily activities. So, an ARG is sort of like gamification.

An ARG Is Transmedia

While ARGs can be differentiated from other digital media experiences, they can contain elements of all media. As a result, ARGs are a *transmedia experience*, an experience that takes place across multiple platforms, formats, and locations. There are elements of eLearning, computer games, geocaching, scavenger hunts, live action role-playing, and social learning. But, an ARG is not one of those activities exclusively. An ARG can be what you need it to be to fit your audience, your goals, your culture, and your creativity. That's the great thing about ARGs. They are flexible gameplay environments that not only can be custom designed but can be adjusted during gameplay to react to the way in which players play the game.

THE LEARNING CONNECTION

The active, problem-based, and social experience in ARGs supports constructivist learning theories, which is one of the reasons why ARGs (and many serious games in general) make great learning environments. Active learning occurs in the learner-centered ARG experience through interpreting clues, solving puzzles, completing scenarios, and engaging in other problem-based learning activities. Learning is more deeply constructed by learners as they interact and collaborate with peers to complete ARG activities. Some ARGs also present opportunities for participants to create content that impacts the experience of other players. The "player as author" concept connects with the "learner as teacher" concept, a constructivist tenet. Essentially, participants learn the most when they are constructing learning (or presentation) for other learners. As any instructional designer can tell you, the person who often learns the most is the creator of the instructional solution. There are still concepts from training on autism monitoring, heavy equipment features, drug formulation, and *[insert your topic]* designs created as an instructional designer that can be recalled many, many, many years later.

The **multimodal** ARG environment also creates learning benefits. Players can experience and interact with concepts in a variety of formats: text, audio, animation, video, social media, etc. The multimodal experience creates variety, which can enhance learner attention and motivation, as well as present opportunities to meet the learning preferences of all participants. The multimodal ARG design also presents opportunities to use the best medium for the message, perhaps even print or live actors depending on the communication goal and gameplay environment.

An ARG can be a powerful learning tool regardless of the domain and level of learning that you are targeting. The most popular model for representing desired learning behaviors and outcomes is Bloom's taxonomy. The most highly referenced domain in Bloom's taxonomy is the cognitive domain with the remembering, understanding, applying, analyzing, evaluating, and creating levels represented in a pyramid like that in Figure 1.1. While not as widely referenced, there are Bloom's taxonomies for the

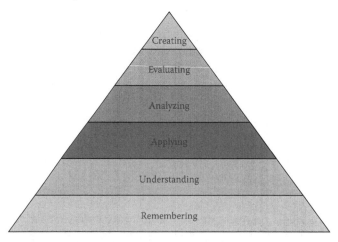

FIGURE 1.1   Bloom's taxonomy (cognitive domain).

TABLE 1.2   Bloom's Taxonomies (All Domains) and the Potential in the ARG Experience

ARG Gameplay for Cognitive (Mental Processes)	ARG Gameplay for Affective (Emotion and Attitude)	ARG Gameplay for Psychomotor (Physical)
Creating: Building new models, processes, or interpretations as part of gameplay	**Characterizing:** Performing with a new attitude in situations in the game where reverting to previous attitudes may be easier	**Originating:** Creating new, more efficient or effective physical approaches (individually or as a team) to complete tasks or achieve goals
Evaluating: Critiquing artifacts, examples, and case studies to consider alternate solutions and/or identify future outcomes	**Organizing:** Creating an individual or team-based action plan for implementing and monitoring attitude change	**Adapting:** Modifying physical actions based on variables presented within the context of gameplay
Analyzing: Determining the best solution among multiple solutions in case studies within the game	**Valuing:** Debating an alternate point of view from either another player or team in the game or a third-party non-player debater	**Mechanizing:** Combining separate movements into a contiguous physical movement (either individually or as a group)
Applying: Practicing concepts in real-world or digital *mini-games* or simulations	**Responding:** Pledging to challenge convention and explore new possibilities within gameplay	**Guided Responding:** Modeling the physical activity required to perform in a game activity (e.g., painting the fence in the movie *The Karate Kid*)
Understanding: Solving puzzles and cryptographs, or playing simple games	**Receiving:** Listening to pro and/or con stories from those who have adopted/adapted the targeted attitudes	**Setting:** Preparing for physical activity by completing a scavenger hunt to gather all of the tools needed
Remembering: Recalling facts in clues as part of gameplay		**Perceiving:** Identifying the most effective and efficient steps and actions by observing

affective (feeling) and psychomotor (physical) domains as well. Table 1.2 indicates how ARGs can potentially have an impact on learning across Bloom's taxonomy levels of learning and learning domains. While it's unlikely that a single ARG will provide experience in all levels of learning across all domains, the table is intended to present the possibilities of addressing Bloom's taxonomies' levels of learning in an ARG.

Better than meeting the expectations of traditional models of education based on Bloom's taxonomies is the ARG's ability to connect to new

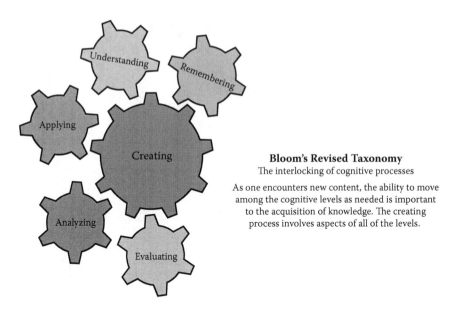

Bloom's Revised Taxonomy
The interlocking of cognitive processes

As one encounters new content, the ability to move among the cognitive levels as needed is important to the acquisition of knowledge. The creating process involves aspects of all of the levels.

FIGURE 1.2 Schrock's gears.

learning design paradigms. One such paradigm shift is represented in the Schrock's gears interpretation of Bloom's cognitive taxonomy (see Figure 1.2). Whereas traditional applications of Bloom's cognitive taxonomy put emphasis on remembering before understanding, before applying, before analyzing, before evaluating, and before creating, Schrock's gears[1] represent creating as the primary cog around which all other levels of learning can be experienced. The gears represent a more fluid movement among the levels of learning throughout the learning experience, versus a linear approach to learning, one level before the next. The problem- and story-based nature of ARGs creates opportunities for a more fluid movement among the levels of learning, versus starting with didactic learning and ending with creation of new concepts or products (if there's even time left for participants to create at the end of the training).

THE BUSINESS APPLICATIONS

An ARG for training or performance improvement should start with … a goal! Establishing a performance goal and learning objectives is the key to any behavior change solution. An ARG is no different. The goal and learning objectives should drive the design of the ARG experience. The game should be fun and unique, but it also needs to be efficient and effective. Don't lose track of your goals and objectives throughout the process.

Why would your business want to implement an ARG? It depends.

- What challenges are you trying to address?
- What is not working with your current orientation or training formats?
- What benefits can you realize from collaboration among employees?
- What challenges are you facing with engaging your customers?

Almost every organization is struggling with overcoming the challenges of time and distance for training initiatives. Many have turned to eLearning or online learning to overcome the challenges that are part of modern business where employees are spread across the globe and time for training is difficult to manage. However, most online learning is a very content-focused and very isolated experience. Organizations looking to get more out of their eLearning initiatives might consider ARGs for developing and practicing skills in training and for promoting the collaboration and networking that takes place in an ARG. In addition, developing skills takes time. By embedding the learning throughout the workday in an ARG, participants have more time to practice over an extended period of time, versus sitting down for a one-hour online learning experience only.

Employee engagement is another challenge that most organizations are facing. Games can engage employees in the organizational goals and their own personal development in ways that other mediums cannot. Games present incremental challenges and ongoing feedback that increase motivation and self-efficacy. An ARG can be an embedded experience that extends the life and benefits of the game-based approach, resulting in longer-term engagement and success. An ARG cannot be the only tool in an engagement strategy, but it can be a very immersive way to kick off an engagement campaign or onboard new employees to increase the level of engagement at the beginning of employment. ARGs for employee engagement will be explored more in Chapter 2.

Innovation is another challenge in today's workplace. An ARG can free the workplace from the shackles of the established training design, implementation, and completion, potentially inspiring innovative thinking at all levels of the organization. The design team will think differently about training solutions. Employees will think differently about learning. New connections will be made throughout the organization as a result of networking in the game. The game itself might even focus on solving a real business problem, leading to idea generation in the game that can be applied to improve the organization.

So if you are negotiating with aliens during sales training someday, you are most likely participating in an ARG. Otherwise, the invasion has begun! As you've read, ARGs are dynamic, transmedia experiences that can be channeled for increased engagement, learning, and collaboration. They can be singular, focused implementations or organization-wide initiatives used to address the employee skill and performance challenges that many organizations face.

ENDNOTES

[1] http://bit.ly/1_BloomingApps

[2] Koreen Olbrish Pagano, *Immersive Learning: Designing for Authentic Practice*, ASTD Press, 2013

[3] Stan Friedman, "Finding the Future: Inside the New York Public Library's All-Night Scavenger Hunt," *Library Journal*, July 2011

[4] Ben Betts, "Spring Revival: Alternate Reality Game Breathes New Life into Old Course," *Learning Solutions Magazine*, January 17, 2011

CHAPTER 2

New Employees Should Be Finding the CEO

Imagine new employees at your organization working as a team to find the missing company CEO, versus sitting all day listening to presentations about the company culture, the organizational structure, and code of conduct expectations. Instead, the search for the CEO requires investigating the company culture, organizational structure, and code of conduct versus hearing about it. How much more engaged do you think the new hires will be? Do you think a highly immersive orientation experience might affirm their decision to work for your organization?

Replacing a single employee can cost about 1-1/2 times the annual salary of the employee being replaced.[1] These costs can include time and money associated with lost productivity, advertising, human resources, and onboarding. Yet, even in tough economic times, organizations regularly see some of the best talent and potential walk out the door, sometimes shortly after joining the organization. Consider some of these statistics:

- 70% of US workers are not engaged at work.[2]

- Only 40% of the workforce *knows* about their company's goals, strategies, and tactics.[3]

- 89% of employers think their people leave for more money, while only 12% of employees do leave for more money.[4]

- Highly engaged employees were 87% less likely to leave their companies than their disengaged counterparts.[5]

- 90% of leaders think an engagement strategy will have an impact on business success, but barely 25% of them have a strategy.[6]

- Companies with actively engaged employees have 2.5 times the revenue versus competitors that have low engagement levels.[7]

Engagement is a multifaceted element of employer-employee relations, and it's not easily addressed. However, alternate reality games (ARGs) can be a tool in the employee engagement strategy. Seventy percent of Forbes global 2000 companies will use gamification to boost engagement, retention, and revenues.[8] ARGs are a form of gamification, one that intersects the boundaries between playing a game and performing daily activities like attending employee orientation, collaborating with a team, or selling products.

Table 2.1 presents some scenarios for using ARGs to increase employee engagement, increase collaboration, optimize training time, develop skills, and fuel innovation.

These scenarios present the potential for ARGs as a solution for a variety of business challenges. Next we'll evaluate a number of ARGs, review the experience and the impact, and consider how your organization might benefit from a similar type of ARG.

ARG 1: IMMERSION INTO NEW PROGRAMS

Designed to give a solid foundation in business concepts to those without a business degree, the Postgraduate Diploma in Applied Management at Warwick Business School (UK) provides an entry-level business management qualification.[9] Participants are often from middle to senior management with at least a few years of management experience who may not be quite ready for an MBA. The undergraduate level diploma requires 23 days of on-site activity over 15 months.

Participants engage in an induction week at the beginning of the diploma program. The induction week is focused on immersion and getting students excited about learning the models and theories they'll be exploring.

TABLE 2.1   Potential ARG Scenarios

Goal	Potential ARG Scenario	Potential Outcomes
Increase New Employee Engagement	New employees at a health care insurance company must find the "Keith the Claim" character and follow him throughout the building to help Keith fulfill his destiny to become a completed claim. Along the way, new employees research information, ask questions of current employees, and create a story that details the life and times of "Keith the Claim."	• Energize employee orientation • Engage new employees • Increase knowledge of the company's business • Increase ability to navigate the facility • Include physical activity during orientation • Generate collaboration between new and existing employees • Evaluate new employees' problem-solving and leadership skills for targeting future leaders
Increase Teamwork and Collaboration	Employees create a Knowledge Management taxonomy that is the basis for a new language that will allow humans and robots to work together.	• Increase collaboration around a mission-critical but challenging task • Increase buy-in and ownership of a new initiative • Leverage the work of a crowd playing a game for efficient productivity
Optimize Training Time	A month prior to safety training, staff members are asked to identify the common thread among several accidents at a production facility. Are they sabotage, faulty equipment, inaccurate safety procedures, inattentive workers, or something even more dangerous? Employees keep a log and a list of "who dun-its" as they investigate safety incidents and bring the materials for use during the safety training.	• Increase context and value of training • Increase engagement in training related to safety outcomes • Establish critical thinking around safety evaluation and activities • Create conversations among employees before training • Allow employee performance in the game to inform the focus of training activities
Increase Skills	Salespeople try to uncover the identity of the perfect customer by researching data and sharing stories with each other about what qualities make a good prospect.	• Increase communication and collaboration among the sales team • Share information about strategies and techniques for the most successful client relationships • Increase the efficiency of sales efforts by identifying ways for salespeople to prioritize prospects

Continued

TABLE 2.1 (*Continued*)   Potential ARG Scenarios

Goal	Potential ARG Scenario	Potential Outcomes
Fuel Innovation	Prior to a national managers meeting, it's announced that the company is moving the corporate offices to Mars as part of a worldwide re-colonization effort. The managers must submit ideas for how the company will establish itself and consider changes in facilities, organizational structure, operations, products— everything the company does.	• Engage managers in innovative thinking before the national meeting • Generate innovative ideas that can be applied to improving the current operations • Identify challenges in the company that might otherwise go unnoticed • Identify opportunities for collaboration among managers with similar ideas

While the induction week and the diploma had been successful, the director of executive education wanted to update the traditional approach. The vision included collaborative learning while simulating the management of a business in a live game environment. An alternate reality game! The game, *Spring Fling*, was played over four days and was based around a failing water cooler company. The players accessed a company website, corresponded with virtual employee characters that had working emails, called live telephone lines, and interacted with live actors in the role of employees and leadership.[10]

The **rabbit hole** was a "future view" video that showed the bankrupt future of the company if changes weren't made. Teams were created and given a USB drive with an executive briefing, company information, and information about services they could purchase to support their work to save the failing company. Players worked together in their teams to create a rescue plan for the company and present the plan to the board. Critical thinking, analysis, exploration, and collaboration were all part of the experience—a fun, busy, fast-moving format that allowed participants to discover concepts and their passion for them.

Does this sound like a learning solution that can be applied to new employee orientation, new salesperson training, or new manager training to create energy and motivation for learning new skills?

The *rabbit hole* is the means by which players become part of the game. It is the "hook" into the game.

ARG 2: TEAMWORK AND COLLABORATIVE NARRATIVE

Five hundred (500) participants, selected from 5,000 applicants, assembled at the New York Public Library (NYPL) to create essays about 100 library artifacts, culminating in a printed book focused on "ways to make history and change the future."[11] The focus of the 12-hour alternate reality game (*Find the Future*) was to find inspiration in creating the future from the historical pioneers and innovators that now live within the archives at the NYPL.

Players self-selected into two teams. Those teams broke into sub-squads to find library artifacts that had been tagged with a **QR code**. When a tagged artifact was found, the squad leader scanned the QR code with the game's mobile app. Found artifacts were logged on a game website where players could view presentations of found artifacts and reveal a related essay assignment, focused on how the past and future are intertwined. Charts on easels, library tours, and hand-delivered messages were part of the game as were the website, Facebook posts, texts, emails, Google docs, Tweets, and Flickr tags. Five hundred (500) essays were written about 100 artifacts and combined into a single printed book that all the participants signed. The book is housed at the library in perpetuity.

A QR or Quick Response Code is a two-dimensional barcode. When scanned by a QR Code Reader, an application on a mobile device with a camera, information is displayed including text, a website URL, a phone number, audio, or video.

Does this sound like an approach that can be applied to knowledge management, creating taxonomies, or writing standard operating procedures?

ARG 3: OPTIMIZE TRAINING TIME

An alternate reality game can be part of a **blended learning** approach. Compared to common approaches like pre-reading or watching videos, an ARG provides a highly immersive and engaging way for learners to prepare for a face-to-face training event. Increased motivation and context for the training event, as well as optimizing the time for the live event, are a few benefits. Learners arriving prepared to participate can optimize training time. Coming with common prior knowledge and having a stake in the outcomes of the event through continued gameplay can increase motivation.

Blended learning originated as online learning components in support of face-to-face training. It has evolved to signify any blend of training modes including online learning as a primary component of the training experience, supported by face-to-face training for group discussion and live role-playing.

Constellation Academy of Wine used an alternate reality game as part of a three-week-long training solution culminating with their national sales meeting.[12] The inside and outside salespeople were presented with a fictional hotel customer including a narrative that described the characteristics of the hotel, specific target customers, room designs, menus, wine lists, and sales data. The learners interacted with customer characters as part of the storyline, including impromptu interaction with the non-player character Facebook pages. Not only did players receive clues from the non-player characters' Facebook posts as part of gameplay, but players also began online conversations with the non-player characters for deeper exploration and learning. The data analysis, relationship building, and sales skills practiced in the ARG extended into the sales meeting and created momentum that would not have been possible with just the sales meeting alone.

Could your face-to-face sales and leadership meetings be optimized by preparing participants prior to the event, establishing common prior knowledge, and building momentum for interaction and collaboration at the event?

ARG 4: INCREASED SKILLS

How do you learn to build and maintain better relationships? You play an alternate reality game! At least that's what students at the University of North Carolina did in a game designed by the School of Information and Library Science and the Student Affairs Department.[13] The goals of the experience were for students to recognize the benefits and drawbacks of involving parents and best friends in relationships, balance privacy and social media use, consider compromise and negotiation as a couple, and reflect on adult decision-making compared to young adulthood decision processes.

ShBANGE (*Should Brandon and Nicole Get Engaged?*) focused on a stressed romantic relationship between two hypothetical students. The game took place over two weeks and included puzzles, online content, videos, Facebook posts, a staged marriage proposal, supporting characters, flyers, balloons, fortune cookies, and a Google Voice number. Players followed the storyline by uncovering clues and information online and throughout campus. As they advanced in the game, players offered relationship suggestions, contributed to wedding plans, and provided general support. The game ended with a party and reflection session where players shared thoughts on and resolutions for the relationship issues witnessed in the game.

In addition to analysis and critical thinking about relationships, privacy, and compromise, information literacy and research skills were also developed through gameplay. Players learned how to locate information using a variety of media and how to share information using similar techniques.

Could observation, practice, and reflection increase your employees' communication, negotiation, conflict resolution, or project management skills?

FUELING INNOVATION AND OTHER ORGANIZATIONAL BENEFITS

Revolutionary breakthroughs are few and far between. More often innovation happens every day and results in refinement instead of revolution. Regardless, innovation is about new ideas and methods. How does your company generate new approaches to everyday challenges? Experiencing new ideas and methods often generates new ideas and methods. With that perspective, alternate reality games can be a way to fuel innovation in an organization. Whether a new training method, new opportunities for collaboration, or new perspectives through the lens of gameplay, ARGs can be a fertile space for leaders, designers, and players to innovate. Table 2.2 indicates the organizational innovation that occurred for each of the ARGs profiled.

TABLE 2.2   Innovation in ARGs

ARG	Innovation
Warwick Business School: *Spring Fling*	Problem-based learning and collaboration was an introduction to learning, versus a conclusion.
New York Public Library: *Find the Future*	A summative and predictive narrative was crowdsourced by 500 players.
Constellation Wine Academy: *Que Syrah Syrah*	Online dialogue with fictional characters led to deeper knowledge and practice.
University of North Carolina: *ShBANGE*	Topics difficult to discuss were explored in an open and collaborative manner.

Crowdsourcing is where small contributions from each member of a large group result in a service, idea, content, or innovation that could not have otherwise been created by only one member of the group.

Other overarching benefits of ARGs include increased learning context, increased learning exposure, and physical activity. Like many immersive learning solutions, ARGs create context for learning. A survey of learning and development professionals indicated that only 34% of trainees apply what they've learned to the workplace one year after a training intervention.[14] Without context, content is passive, disconnected, and not likely to have an impact on workplace performance. When learners see the connection between content and their work through immersive learning like ARGs, they are more likely to transfer the skills they develop to the workplace.

Learning doesn't happen at a moment in time. New knowledge, skills, and attitudes are built over extended periods of exploration, practice, feedback, and reflection. Most classroom and online training is designed as a one-hour, one-day, or one-week experience that takes the learner away from the workplace. As described in some of the examples, ARGs can be integrated into work and life activities throughout the day and take place over an extended period of time. Assimilating learning into work can create an atmosphere where there is no difference between the two, where employees are always working and always learning (a learning organization).

From stress reduction and smoking cessation programs to stand-up desks and digital health monitors, organizations are looking to improve the health of their workforce. Lower insurance costs, increased productivity, and improved morale can be results. Getting up, out of a chair, and moving has health and physiological cognitive benefits that can impact learning and performance. ARGs can be a great way to increase movement as participants walk around spaces to find clues, ask questions, and collaborate on problem solving.

FULL PARTICIPATION

In Chapter 1, an ARG experience was described as one in which "the realism of the story is strong at the beginning and the player might not be sure whether they are even playing a game." That is a good description of the experience in an entertainment or educational ARG where 100% target audience participation is *not* required. In those instances, the ARG is often a tangential experience that enhances the main entertainment or learning objective. However, in business and education 100% target audience participation and completion is often necessary.

In the *Spring Fling* ARG at Warwick Business School participants were gathered specifically for the purpose of induction into the certificate program. The rabbit hole was a video that was presented to everyone. Story materials were directly given to participants and teams were coordinated to launch the game. The beginning gameplay was still subtle, but the story and directions were overt at the beginning so that full participation would result.

The *Find the Future* ARG for the New York Public Library gained full participation by requiring players to apply to participate. From over 5,000 applicants, 500 players were selected. The intrinsic motivation to participate was generated by the exclusivity of the event. While this doesn't demonstrate 100% participation of the target audience of 5,000, it does demonstrate a way to select a segment of the target audience from which full participation will result. This approach may be a good option for leadership training or other company-wide initiatives that don't require 100% of the employee population to participate but do require full participation from those selected.

Que Syrah Syrah for Constellation Wine Academy did not include 100% participation by the target audience. While a high participation rate was achieved (84%), it was not required that everyone take part in the ARG. Those that didn't participate in the ARG simply participated in the sales conference as they normally would. *ShBANGE* at the University of North Carolina also did not achieve 100% target audience participation.

Forced participation in gameplay is counterintuitive. People play games because they want to. They are intrinsically motivated to play because they want to have fun, love the storyline, or connect with the characters. Forcing participation in an ARG from the top-down—"You will play this game! You will have fun! You will learn something!"—is a sure recipe for failure. Not to mention, it's counterproductive to morale, employee engagement, and learner-centered experiences.

If you need 100% target audience participation in your ARG for business or education, there are any number of ways that you can do so. You can use strategies like those used in *Spring Fling* or *Find the Future*. You can also apply strategies like multiple rabbit holes, the buddy system, or bait-and-switch to achieve 100% participation.

MULTIPLE RABBIT HOLES

Remember that an ARG is built around a story that often initially engages the player through an anomaly in their regular schedule. Like when Alice stumbles into the world of Wonderland through the literal rabbit hole, the hook into the story and the game is the *rabbit hole*. An ARG rabbit hole can be almost anything: an email from an unknown source, a Post-it note on a desk, or a video. The subtle entry into gameplay can be a challenge when targeting 100% participation. Not all of the target audience will recognize the rabbit hole or, if they recognize it, respond to it. Traditionally ARGs have one rabbit hole into the game. A way of increasing participation in a business or education ARG is to create multiple points of entry into gameplay—multiple rabbit holes. What if Alice hadn't tumbled down the one rabbit hole along the path? We wouldn't know about the Queen of Hearts or the Mad Hatter. But, if there are a field of rabbit holes, Alice's chances of meeting the Queen are infinitely increased. Multiple rabbit holes could take the form of the same message in multiple locations and/or formats. Or, you can get creative and enhance the story by creating multiple, but unique, rabbit holes for the player to get engaged with the game.

THE BUDDY SYSTEM

Bring a friend! Another way of increasing participation to 100% is to ask players who are engaged in the game to bring someone else along for the ride. As part of the rabbit hole or during early gameplay, encourage players to find someone who's not currently playing and bring him or her into the experience. *Farmville* on Facebook saw tremendous growth from 2009 to 2012 as a result of "the buddy system." A mechanic of the *Farmville* game is to give points and bonus access to items you need to grow your farm for inviting new players into the game.[15] If you are designing an ARG on improving trust in the organization, you might ask players to "find someone who's currently not on the Trust Train and invite them on board at the next stop." Or, if you are designing an ARG for Principles of Auditing, you might require each player to begin the game with a person to audit their performance. There are a variety of scenarios that can make the buddy system work for increasing participation in an ARG.

BAIT-AND-SWITCH

Imagine sitting down at your computer to complete the yearly safety compliance training. Halfway through the training your computer screen is "hijacked" by a video message from someone in research and development who wants you to help her make a new product safe before the company's reputation is irrevocably damaged. Or, imagine you're sitting in a training room for a session on sustainability and the president of the company barges in to announce a challenge at a plant in Wichita that needs to be addressed right away. If 100% participation is expected for the traditional training experience, use that as an advantage and a gateway for gaining 100% participation in the ARG. By hijacking the traditional training approach with entry into the ARG, you create a rabbit hole that is difficult to ignore. In the end, the participants will most likely thank you for saving them from traditional training with the bait-and-switch.

Ultimately, there will always be someone who doesn't want to play the game no matter how many rabbit holes you place in front of them. There are also employees and students who may not be able to play because of an injury, a medical condition, or a disability. An option should exist for those employees, too. You might be able to turn your ARG script into a document that they can read. You can package the ARG media and activities into a traditional format. That may take the form of a "walkthrough" where a guide explains and presents the ARG step-by-step as learners observe the story. A guide can also serve as a resource and support as "walkthrough learners" complete ARG activities and challenges outside of the main gameplay. Or, you can offer a traditional format as you would have offered it originally. Over time, and with some of the strategies outlined here, the nonparticipants will be a small group. But, they are still a part of your audience that you need to consider if 100% participation and completion is needed.

You can see the variety of ways in which ARGs can meet organizational, knowledge, and performance challenges. As you consider an ARG for your next training initiative, remember to capture the innovative practices that the format allows and don't forget to create accommodations to achieve 100% target audience participation, if it's required.

ENDNOTES

[1] Employee Recruiting Costs versus Employee Retention—http://bit.ly/2_EmployeeCosts
[2] 70% of U.S. Workers Not Engaged at Work—http://bit.ly/2_USWorkplace
[3] 20 Shocking HR Statistics—http://bit.ly/2_HRstats
[4] The 7 Hidden Reasons Employees Leave—http://bit.ly/2_LeaveReasons
[5] 20 Interesting Employee Engagement Facts and Figures—http://bit.ly/2_EmployeeFacts
[6] Building a Culture of Engagement—http://bit.ly/2_DaleCarnegie
[7] 10 Shocking Stats about Disengaged Employees—http://bit.ly/2_TenStats
[8] Gartner predicts over 70 percent of global 2000 organizations will have at least one gamified application by 2014—http://bit.ly/2_Gartner

[9] Ben Betts, "Spring Revival: Alternate Reality Game Breathes New Life into Old Course," *Learning Solutions Magazine*, January 17, 2011

[10] Campden Springs website—http://bit.ly/2_CampdenSprings

[11] Stan Friedman, "Finding the Future: Inside the New York Public Library's All-Night Scavenger Hunt," *Library Journal*, July 2011

[12] Immersive Learning: Designing for Authentic Practice—http://bit.ly/2_ImmersiveLearning

[13] Should Brandon and Nicole Get Engaged?—http://bit.ly/2_ShBANGE

[14] How Your Workplace Can Support Learning Transfer—http://bit.ly/2_LearningTransfer

[15] Gamification Research: How *FarmVille* Uses Game Mechanics to Become Winning & Addicting—http://bit.ly/2_FarmVilleAddict

CHAPTER 3

Keeping Up
with the Joneses

The title of this chapter is an idiom that refers to comparing one's accumulated material goods and social class to that of others. Usually, it's an unfair apples-to-oranges comparison but one that many fall in to. We are going to examine profiles of a few ARGs to get a feel for the "neighborhood" and see who is doing what. This will not be an extensive examination; instead we will identify various components of the ARG experience as a method of determining how one could be implemented in your organization.

ARGs are used to tackle many different challenges—from product releases, training and mentoring, to nontraditional entertainment. Consequently, ARGs appear in many forms based on the overall objectives, platforms, and method of execution necessary at the intersection of technology, location, audience, and story. In this chapter we'll explore the gameplay, platforms, and activities of five ARGs from various public and private sources. Comparing ARGs is problematic because, as stated in Chapter 1, each one has its own unique design and player experiences, which have been developed to achieve specific goals. In Chapter 4 we'll spend more time discussing the development process, but here we are summarizing a few examples to gain a deeper understanding of the motivations, methods, and outcomes of the projects. These examples, presented in order of complexity, were chosen because of their different approaches to delivering unique user experiences. Beyond these ARG profiles, the Alternate Reality Gaming Network[1] and other similar ARG repositories are great resources for ideas and innovations in the ARG community.

TABLE 3.1   ARG Profiles: *Robots Are Eating the Building*

Robots Are Eating the Building	
Premise	In *Robots Are Eating the Building* a cohort of small devious robots are destroying the main academic tower of Harrisburg University. No one knows their ultimate goal, but the destruction at the start of the "Learning and Entertainment Evolution Forum" was not part of the planning committee's schedule. It was quickly determined that these sentient beings can be defeated by acquiring and uploading specific bits of data to the building's network, effectively overloading the robot's memory causing them to be disabled.
Sponsor/Developer	Center for Advanced Entertainment and Learning Technologies, Harrisburg University
Purpose	Provide networking and career exploration activities for learning and entertainment conference attendees.
Gameplay	This ARG was conducted at the Learning and Entertainment Evolution Forum at Harrisburg University in the spring of 2010. A few days before the event, CCTV footage was released to the website showing how five robots were destroying the building, one room at a time. The video concluded with a call-to-action for conference attendees. The video was also played during the conference's opening session. When participants arrived and picked up their badges they were offered five game cards that identified a variety of optional networking challenges for conference attendees. Each card identified one of five robots to be defeated over the two-day conference.
	Players could deactivate a robot by providing answers to challenges identified on the cards. Some robots were tougher than others requiring four or five facts about attendees, while most were easily dispatched with one or two details. Players used downtime between sessions, the lunch hour, and designated breaks to locate attendees who matched the specific criteria needed to defeat a robot's components. As an example, let's look at the ID Bot illustrated in Figure 3.1. This robot card represented the field of instructional design. It had three working components: a range sensor, a controller, and traction actuators, which needed to be deactivated to incapacitate the robot. Supplying an answer to a challenge question would deactivate the component. Below are the actual questions needed for the ID Bot: • Identify someone who has "instructional design" in their job title to disable the ID Bot's range sensor. (This was a common job title among attendees.) • Identify someone who does instructional design for military projects to disable the ID Bot's main controller (~20% of the attendees fit this combination of skills).

TABLE 3.1 (*Continued*) ARG Profiles: *Robots Are Eating the Building*

	• Identify an instructional designer with the first initial *R* to disable the ID Bot's traction motor actuator. (Only 2 of the 84 attendees fit this criteria.)
	Players who completed all five cards were eligible for a drawing hosted during the final session of the two-day conference.
Platforms	• This game was played using physical game cards that identified challenges and served as the progression mechanism.
	• A game-master was also on hand to assist with challenges and collect/score game cards.
	• Gameplay took place across three floors of the academic tower.
Activities	Paper game cards; professional networking; social learning (no digital interactions)
Expected outcomes	This activity promoted professional networking and introduced the concept of "games for professional development" to conference attendees. Participants made contacts with other learning technologists.
Time frame	Two days; June 17–18, 2010
Participants	75–80

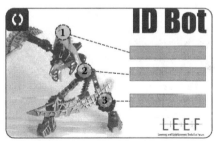

Front

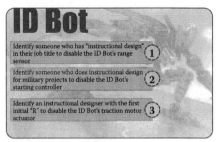

Back

FIGURE 3.1 ID Bot card.

TABLE 3.2   ARG Profiles: *I Love Trees*

I Love Trees	
Premise	PETE&C is an annual conference for educators and administrators to meet and discuss strategies, technologies, and the resources needed to effectively use technology in education. The *I Love Trees* ARG focused on helping participants develop their own powerful learning practices (PLP) while attending the conference. Players took on the role of a new principal at West Side High, whose superintendent has asked for research on PLP and to determine how the techniques can be integrated into the school district. Players were tasked with growing the school's tree of knowledge by advancing their understanding of PLP.
Sponsor	Pennsylvania Educational Technology Expo and Conference (PETE&C)
Purpose	The project had two concrete goals: (1) create pre-conference experience to engage attendees, (2) introduce educators to the ideas and concepts behind PLP, a year-long method of educating instructors on how technology can enhance teaching and learning.
	Players were introduced to the game via a Twitter post using the #petec11 hashtag. Email announcements were also sent out to conference registrants prior to and at the beginning of the conference.
Gameplay	PETE&C participants registered at the game's website. Once registered, individuals were given a digital PLP sapling (Figure 3.2) that would grow as the player answered questions and found clues hidden throughout the exhibit hall. Clues were found among the tweeted messages from Superintendent Wiggins, in placards and signs, in session materials provided by conference speakers, with exhibitors, and if they were lucky from Superintendent Wiggins himself portrayed by Justin Detig, an HU instructional designer and media producer (Figure 3.3).
	The ARG's website served as the primary communication vehicle for the game. Aside from collecting and validating player answers, the site also had an archive of Tweets, game hints, instructions about playing the game, and a leaderboard where players could celebrate their achievements and check on their progress.
Platforms	• Website built with WordPress, customized to facilitate user progress and integrated with content from Twitter and YouTube
	• Gameplay made ample use of the exhibit halls, session rooms, and vendor booths of the conference facility
	• Activities were managed by two staff members and an actor portraying Superintendent Wiggins
Activities	Website (primarily mobile), direct email, public Twitter feed, introductory video, placards with QR codes and cryptograms, and a live actor were used to educate participants about PLP and digital learning opportunities to integrate into the classroom and the district.

TABLE 3.2 (*Continued*)   ARG Profiles: *I Love Trees*

Outcomes	Participants increased their knowledge of digital teaching and learning practices and of the PLP framework and networked among peers.
Time frame	Two days; Feb. 12–13, 2011
Participants	151 registered, 82 active, 22 highly active
More information	See the debrief on SlideShare—http://bit.ly/3_ILT

FIGURE 3.2   PLP progression bar growing from sapling to full tree.

FIGURE 3.3   Superintendent Wiggins from the *I Love Trees* ARG.

TABLE 3.3   ARG Profiles: *Blink Mining*

Blink Mining	
Premise	Evidence shows that simulation-based training significantly enhances team-level competencies during critical non-routine events and can be particularly effective in business education. The goal of *Blink Mining* was to provide a mechanism for teaching crisis management to university students.
Developer	Professor Mary Waller, Ph.D., Schulich School of Business, York University
Purpose	Provide a team-based crisis management and disaster recovery simulation to study and assess team dynamics.
Gameplay	This two-hour intensive simulation puts teams of participants in the role of C-level executives who have to react to a stressful scenario where critical decisions must be made every 10 minutes based on a limited amount of information revealed to each player over the course of the experience. During the game, players must communicate with their team and stakeholders of the fictitious company while addressing the unfolding crisis.
	The scenario begins with an email from Blink Mining's general manager; the mine has received a bomb threat and the CEO is on a commercial flight and won't be available for the next two hours. It is the player's job to work with their executive team to make key decisions about the crisis. As messages from angry investors, inquiring reporters, company employees, and concerned government officials start arriving via email, direct texts, and social media, new permutations of the crisis emerge requiring the player to collaborate and respond quickly to the growing threat.
	All messages and communications in the ARG are managed and delivered using Conducttr,[2] an audience engagement tool used to build immersive, cross-platform experiences.
Platforms	• This classroom ARG relied on Conducttr to manage events, non-player character (NPC) communications, and story pacing • Prof. Waller served as puppet-master during each session • Gameplay took place in a single classroom
Activities	Email, **SMS**, Twitter, and Facebook
Time frame	Two hours
Participants	Up to 35 participants working in seven teams of five students per session
Comments	"I was also surprised at how stressful the students found some intentional 'lulls' in the action that I had inserted in the simulation. They said that the quiet times were as stressful, if not more stressful, than the periods of heavy action. This is one of the ways that the simulation differs from a game; another way is that the students do not have a running 'points' counter or any such clear indication during the simulation of their performance level. Real crises do not come with a scoreboard." <div align="right">—Professor Mary Waller, Ph.D.</div>

TABLE 3.4   ARG Profiles: *Click! Spy Agency*

Click! Spy Agency	
Premise	The *Click!* urban adventure program for middle-school girls was part *Charlie's Angels* and part MTV's *Real World*. In the game, *Click!* agents used specialized tablet computer interfaces, location-aware mobile devices, and digital documentation to engage girls in a six-day summer camp. After five days of training, *Click!* girls had an all-day adventure at Carnegie Science Center. When completed, the girls were awarded second-level agent status.
Sponsor	Carnegie Science Center
Purpose	Introduce young girls to underrepresented STEM careers. In Level 1, attendees conduct experiments, perform scientific research, and use inductive reasoning to solve the case of the perplexing peach. This case focuses on hands-on inquiry to encourage collaborative problem solving and participatory learning. Once completed, the girls graduate to Level 2 and can come back to work on an environmental protection mystery with a new cast of characters and challenges the following summer.
Gameplay	After a week of training (in biomedical engineering, environmental protection, and expressive technologies) the girls come to the final day of camp only to learn that the senior *Click!* agents have been called away on various missions. In their absence a biomedical mystery has been discovered and it's up to the young agents to figure out a solution. The case starts with news that a Pittsburgh Steeler has fallen ill. A small group of girls travels across the street to Heinz Field to interview the team chef about possible foods ingested by the player and gather background information on foodborne illnesses. Another team of *Click!* agents examines case files from other patients and extracts DNA for further study, while yet another team takes their investigation online to learn about how two other local companies (Del Monte and a nearby restaurant) might also be involved in the mystery. Using personal interviews, websites, a science lab, and tablet computers, the girls engage in activities associated with the careers they've been studying all week.
Platforms	• Tablet PCs with a custom interface, a custom social media tool, various websites, science lab • Numerous NPCs playing the role of subject matter experts brought the experience to life. • Gameplay took place within a four-block radius of the Carnegie Science Center's North Shore home.
Activities	Communication skills (interviews with NPCs, social media tool), research (websites), deductive reasoning (documentation)
Time frame	Five hours
Participants	20 middle-school-aged girls

Continued

TABLE 3.4 (*Continued*)   ARG Profiles: *Click! Spy Agency*

More information	In this ARG, the Level 1 participants were really engaged in the storyline—so much so that the girls created their own reality when confronted with alternate/conflicting information. After coming across a ***red herring*** in the storyline, the girls wanted to confirm some information they received from Rachel, the NPC waitress at a local restaurant. Without telling the *Click!* staff, the team found the restaurant's phone number and called asking for the waitress. Of course the waitress was a hired actress using a fake name, and the hostess told the team that no one with that name worked there. This could have presented a real problem, but instead of saying "this is fake" the girls came to the conclusion that the "waitress" must have been hired by the food processing plant to misinform the team. This renewed their efforts to find the culprits responsible in the "perplexing peaches" case.

TABLE 3.5   ARG Profiles: *The Black Watchmen*

The Black Watchmen

Premise	*The Black Watchmen*[3] are a paramilitary group dedicated to protecting the public from dangerous phenomena beyond human understanding: ritualistic murder, occult secret societies, and paranormal activity, to name but a few. As a global organization, *The Black Watchmen* offer a wide range of skills and services for covert missions anywhere in the world, on behalf of any group, corporation, or government that can afford them. Often called in as a last resort, *The Black Watchmen* pride themselves on their discretion, strength, and efficiency.
Developer	Montreal-based Alice & Smith[4]
Purpose	Alice & Smith have set out to create the first permanent ARG. This is less of a game and more of a new reality to be experienced and explored.
Gameplay	Players register and play the game via Steam,[5] an online game platform. After registering, players take on the role of a newly recruited *Black Watchmen* agent using a dashboard dubbed the "Mission Hub" to train and conduct research. The "trainee" missions consist of activities, which highlight online research techniques, being observant, and completing a primer on cryptography. These and future mission-related activities are managed through the Mission Hub, which monitors agent progress, provides research tools, and serves as a central communications hub. The early missions are straightforward but challenging.
	Once training is complete, players can determine the level of immersion they are looking for in the ARG. Each immersion level is represented by a color as outlined below:
	• **Red**: interactions with red level agents will take place through the Mission Hub and via email
	• **Orange**: interactions may include voicemails, live streams
	• **Yellow**: all of the above with phone calls (which might come at any time of the day or night), suspicious packages sent by mail, and interactions with real NPC
	• **Green**: promises to be the highest level of immersion. Details are thin, but a full medical exam and personal injury waiver are required. This level is not for the faint of heart, but if selected, you will remember the experience for the rest of your life.
Platforms	• Primary interaction is through the Mission Hub and emails; additional interactions are possible at higher levels of immersion
	• Most contact with the game world and other players is via online communication; some physical interaction is also expected as research is conducted by agents across the globe
Activities	• The game is played via websites, newspaper ads, phone calls, and text messages and by visiting real-world locations
	• Heavy problem solving requires players working in collaboration. The collaboration is facilitated through the game's Mission Hub, forums, and direct email.
Time frame	Ongoing
Participants	Recently released; 1,908 agents as of July 5, 2015

TABLE 3.6   ARG Profiles: *The Threshold*

The Threshold[6]	
Premise	In a fictional universe, players uncover clues and solve mysteries of an intricately woven story that plunges players into the world of high-stakes corporate espionage.
Developer	No Mimes Media in conjunction with JUXT Interactive and a leading technology company
Purpose	A four-week teamwork and collaboration exercise to engage the company's worldwide employees in preparation for a 2009 sales conference.
Gameplay	To unravel the ARG's mystery, players exchanged emails and voicemail messages with NPCs over the three-week period prior to the global conference. Websites, CCTV-style videos, and even webinars also served as resources for clues and challenges.
Platforms	Company employees from across the global played the game using: • Audio files • Short Message Service (SMS) • Voicemail • Chat rooms • Social media tools • Webinars • Digital posters • Surveillance videos • Websites • Direct email • Virtual meeting spaces • Wikipages • Forums • Hidden messages
Activities	• Played in real-time over four-week period • Various puzzle-solving activities • Virtual visits to remote locations • Collection of player points for real-world prizes (top-scoring team was awarded a Super Bowl getaway)
Time frame	Four weeks in total
Participants	13,000 of 19,000 worldwide conference attendees (double the expected participation)
More information	Read the complete summary and watch the overview video on No Mimes Media's website (http://nomimes.com/)

Although the examples represent a wide range of uses—from middle school age to adults, classrooms to the streets of Chicago, low-tech paper and pencil to highly produced video content and custom applications—they offer a glimpse into the activities and challenges possible in the modern ARG. We'll revisit some of these examples in future chapters, but for now just keep in mind the variety of concepts, technologies, and goals.

OTHER ARGS TO EXPLORE

- The *A.I. Web Game*—An ARG created by a team at Microsoft to promote the film *A.I.: Artificial Intelligence*—http://bit.ly/3_TheBeast

- *Zombie, Run!*—A personal fitness ARG where players run to escape zombies and periodically solve puzzles—http://bit.ly/3_ZombieRun

- *World Without Oil*—popular ARG from noted game designers Jane McGonigal and Ken Eklund—http://bit.ly/3_WWO

ENDNOTES

[1] Alternate Reality Gaming Network—http://bit.ly/3_ARGnet

[2] Immersive storytelling and gaming software for education, entertainment, and marketing—http://bit.ly/3_Conducttr

[3] Backstory and features of *The Black Watchmen* ARG—http://bit.ly/3_TBW

[4] Alice & Smith, the makers of *The Black Watchmen*, is an entertainment company in Montreal, Canada—http://bit.ly/3_AliceAndSmith

[5] Steam is a web-based entertainment platform used to deliver game products and tools—http://bit.ly/3_Steam

[6] A teamwork and collaboration ARG developed by No Mimes Media—http://bit.ly/3_Threshold

CHAPTER 4

All the World Is a Stage

ARGs do not spring fully formed from their creator's mind. Instead, they are the result of many hours of ideation, refinement, and testing—not to mention the setbacks, technical issues, creeping *scope*, interpersonal conflicts, and Excedrin strength headaches that occur. But like any creative endeavor, the reward of seeing your creation come to life and the goals achieved is priceless.

Alternate reality games use complex stories told across multiple media formats to blur the lines between fiction and reality. Each activity, learning objective, technical component, and communication vehicle is evaluated by how it impacts users as they uncover the mystery hidden within the narrative. In our experience, no two ARG developers follow the same development process. But many common approaches and practices are in use.

The most common development practices seem to originate as a cross between the prototypical software development life cycle (SDLC), used in many technology-related industries, the production process used in stage performances, and the Analysis, Design, Development, Implementation, and Evaluation (ADDIE) process used for the design of adult learning solutions. Together, these three production fields (technology, the dramatic arts, and instructional design) emphasize the importance of maintaining a cross-disciplinary approach when building these highly engaging experiences. ARGs are fundamentally team-oriented collaborations, drawing from a wide variety of skill sets, requiring precise execution, while being performed with, or in front of, a live audience.

Specific production steps vary greatly from project to project, but in general the ARG process follows *initiation*, *preproduction*, *production*, and *postproduction* as the primary phases, but is overlapped by SDLC and

TABLE 4.1   ARG Production Milestones across Methodologies

Film/Stage Production	SDLC	ADDIE
Development	Definition	Analysis
	Requirements	
Preproduction	Analysis	Analysis
	Design	Design
Production	Prototype	Design
	Build	Development
	Test	Evaluation
Postproduction	Revisions	Evaluation
	Final testing	Implementation
Go live	Deploy/kickoff	Implementation
	Debrief	Analysis

ADDIE milestones. Table 4.1 lists the milestones for each methodology that impacts on ARG creation and how each methodology supports and augments each other.

With the multitude of moving parts across the phases and milestones, the most important component in building an ARG is developing a coherent plan. The plan is a physical document that will broadly outline the crafting process with specific goals and milestones. It's a living document, which will be updated and revised many times during the production process. And lastly, it serves as an overview document to be archived with the project's artifacts for review by future teams wishing to refine and build a new ARG starting with a familiar approach.

BUILDING AN ARG

For the purposes of this document we will discuss a simplified version of our production process. We have utilized versions of this outline during the development of four ARGs, each time identifying areas of improvement and tweaking as new requirements and technologies are needed. Before tackling your own production we highly suggest you become familiar with this structure and others to build an approach that fits your needs.

1. Initiation

2. Preproduction

    a. Build teams

    b. Define goals, objectives, and preliminary schedule

    c. Design the experience

    d. Document the idea and process

    e. Build a media plan

    f. Put it all together

3. Production

    a. Create a treatment

    b. Build components

    c. Prepare to fail

4. Postproduction

5. Go live

    a. Hosting the game

    b. Starting the game

    c. Monitoring the experience

    d. Ending the game

6. Debrief

INITIATION

This phase is often overlooked as a true project phase, but this is where the ARG idea is formed and defined. At some point the concept of an ARG is initiated and brought to others for discussion. But before preproduction can begin, the individuals responsible for the creative vision should document what they have in mind. In some instances the idea is documented in a formal creative brief or on a napkin during an informal discussion over coffee. But in either case, the goal is to take a root idea and transform it into a governing concept of the ARG itself.

In 2010 Tandem Learning set out to develop an ARG for field sales managers at the Constellation Academy of Wine. The experience needed to illustrate the nuances of the sales process for Constellation employees. To achieve this goal the designers wanted to create an environment where students could safely experience the sales process without working with real clients. The team decided a fictitious hotel would provide the theme and environment for delivering the educational message. Students would practice their sales skills by working in this simulated environment and the training staff could easily review the choices made by each trainee. Once this very basic problem statement is defined, the project lead(s) can use this information to draft the creative brief. This document, along with the addition of a few components outlined below, will be used to kick off the preproduction phase of the project.

Initiation is also where the ARG's requirements are documented. Is the experience primarily being used to educate or entertain? What level of participation is acceptable? What technologies will the players use to interact with the game? When and where will the ARG take place and for how long? Is it repeatable? Do all players begin at the same time or is discovery of the game the first activity? Having a firm understanding of these questions before the preproduction phase will help further the success of the project.

PREPRODUCTION

Build the Teams

As soon as the creative brief is defined and requirements have been established, start building a management team. This is the first of many teams that will be formed to tackle various phases of the project. The management team should be a collection of creative brainstormers, technologists, and stakeholders familiar with the project's target audience. Their goal is to identify the project's objectives, suggest possible team members, and build a rough schedule for production. This team should also establish the communication tools and procedures (physical and digital) needed to facilitate how the creative, technical, and administrative teams will work together. Table 4.2 is a sampling of the sub-teams, their responsibilities, and the relative effort levels.

Of course this is just one of many approaches, but as a guide it illustrates the relationships between teams and provides a rough estimate of their involvement in each phase. It should also be mentioned that team members often move between sub-teams based on individual skills, resources, and schedules. Many teams are so small (2–3 developers) that the lines between duties and responsibility are blurred beyond definition.

Define the Goals, Objectives, and a Preliminary Schedule

Another task for the management team is to determine what a successful ARG will accomplish. What are the ARG's terminal objectives (entertainment, learning, or brand marketing)? Which audiences are to be targeted? What are the desired outcomes of each game activity?

TABLE 4.2   Preproduction Teams and Responsibilities

Team	Effort during Each Phase (Scale of 1 to 4)				
	Initiation	Preproduction	Production	Postproduction	Debrief
Management Determine project objectives, goals, and outcomes	2	3	2	2	3
Design Envision the user and system experience	0	4	2	1	3
Content Create sensory assets (what the player will see, touch, hear, smell, and taste)	0	0	4	4	1
Development Build technical and physical systems to support the user experience	0	2	4	4	3
Quality assurance (QA) Conduct testing and validate project objectives	0	0	2	4	2
Go live Manage users and the overall system during the live gameplay	0	0	0	4	3

In the corporate setting where training or orientation is the primary focus, the team should document the desired behavior changes and skills to be acquired by the participants. In entertainment or marketing ventures, on the other hand, the experience is normally centered on a product release, gathering event, or other marketing challenge where the goal is often part of an awareness campaign within a specific audience. In both cases, the goals and objectives should be documented and this can serve as the basis for the team's *design document*.

Next the management team sets an initial schedule for the project. This schedule is normally built in reverse starting with possible *go-live* dates that are used to extrapolate rough milestones and task durations to determine a kickoff date and overall schedule. Figure 4.1 provides an example of the initial development schedule for the experimental Deep Sleep Initiative, a casual ARG developed by a team of students from Carnegie Mellon University (http://bit.ly/4_ARx). Note that this Gantt chart illustrates a

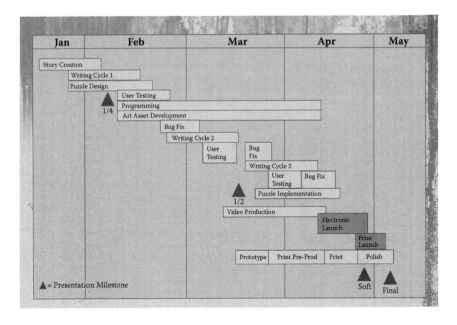

FIGURE 4.1 Production schedule from ARx Deep Sleep Initiative—http://bit.ly/4_ARx.

rough schedule of tasks and activities to be completed over time. It should also be noted that little consideration is given to the game schedule at this time, other than a rough estimate in terms of length (hours, days, or months). Once a schedule of work has been proposed, it can be added to the executive summary in preparation for the next phase of the project.

Design the Experience

The design team is charged with crafting an experience, which will excite, entertain, and motivate the game's players. Starting with the objectives, goals, audience, and proposed schedule outlined by the management team, designing the experience begins with a series of brainstorming sessions, where design and development teams gather to collectively share information and choose a creative direction. Ask yourself and the team:

- · What are we asking the players to do? Solve, create, visit, share, and find are all common activities of ARG players. More about ARG activities will be discussed in Chapter 6.

- What tools will be needed to accomplish these tasks? Internet access, mobile devices, live actors, written and visual materials, QR-code app, or teams are just a few.

- Are there themes and metaphors that will connect the **game objectives** to the desired player behaviors? Don't limit yourself to the mundane; go for the extraordinary. Instead of creating the typical supply chain simulation, have participants serve as advisors to a failing manufacturing company in New Hope, the largest and most profitable colony on Mars.

- Are the skills for building the creative and technical assets readily available?

- Are there any obvious rabbit hole events? It might be a URL hidden within conference materials, a series of broadcast advertisements that on closer review provide latitude and longitude coordinates, a worn and weathered journal left on a park bench, or a keynote presenter overtly announcing the game's beginning. Whichever event is chosen, it should be designed to help set the game's tone with the players.

The outcome of your brainstorming session(s) is to establish the game's thematic scenario and structure, which will let players explore the world and adapt the intended behavior change or engagement presented by the ARG.

Document the Idea and Development Process

After the concept, theme, and structure are defined, the design team will develop the design document. This document can take many forms, but here are some items that should be defined and addressed:

- *Overview*: This section defines the intended purpose of the ARG: why it's being created, who it's for, and what the desired outcomes are.

- *Game objectives*: This can be for the entire project or subdivided for each target audience. Game objectives are important because they also help define success.

- *Story*: This will include theme concept, background story of the world, important characters, key game world events, player roles and motivations.

- *Player experience*: This might list technical requirements, social interactions, and player activities. We often build this by first documenting how the player will interact with the game world, starting with the rabbit hole event and ending with any post-game activities. See Chapter 6 for a detailed look at defining the player experience.

- *Production schedule:* This section includes a breakdown of production tasks as well as an outline of the event-driven activities from the player's perspective.

ARGology[1] is a website devoted to collecting and archiving information for ARG developers. Although the site lacks any recent updates, it still contains hundreds of articles and links about the development process. In particular, the Designing Links section has a number of documents discussing the design and budgeting process.

Build a Media Plan

How will your players find out about the game? How will they communicate within the game world and with each other during gameplay? These are some of the questions you'll need to answer when developing a media plan. The media plan, which will be added to the design document, focuses on the traditional (offline) and digital (online) elements used to deliver content to your players. Tools such as SMS (direct or public broadcast), Twitter, Instagram, YouTube, Facebook, WordPress, Wikis, custom websites, and the like, are common technologies accessible to most ARG audiences via smartphones and tablets. But they should not be the only access point. Traditional items like printed posters, handouts, public announcement systems, and live actors add more than just variety of message delivery; they also keep the less technically savvy players engaged and provide an alternative point of engagement in the event of unexpected technical failures (e.g., Wi-Fi outage, dead batteries).

Put It All Together

Once these components are completed, the design document will serve as a communication vehicle for the production teams. It's used to guide the production phase and will influence the creation of the creative and technical elements needed to craft the intended experience.

PRODUCTION

After defining the project and determining a strategy for completing the work, the development team moves into the production phase. In this phase the team begins producing the written, visual, and programmatic elements needed to interact with players, computing devices, and the general public. These content elements—animation, graphics, music, narration, photography, sound effects, and video footage—are developed using the specifications identified during preproduction and defined in the design document.

Use a Treatment to Prototype the Experience

We often approach the production phase by producing a *treatment*. The treatment, or *alpha test*, is a representative component of the ARG that might contain a mix of various elements. It lets the team "test" their design assumptions from the previous phase before moving into full production mode.

In *The Pocket* ARG, our players were Pennsylvania educators attending a conference in the winter of 2012. The goal of *The Pocket* game was to help educators understand the benefits of Bring Your Own Technology (BYOT) programs being piloted across the country. Attendees were encouraged to think differently about the incredible computing power many students have in their pockets instead of viewing the devices as distractions. Our treatment was a portion of gameplay that served as the basis of the ARG experience the teachers would have at the conference. During the event, players needed to decipher answers from game clues and submit them to the game system. The game system would then validate the clue code and, if applicable, apply points to the players' accounts and advance their virtual avatar on a game board. So, for the treatment we identified the following needs:

- Two game clues (of the 45 total clues):
  - A physical clue to be included in print material. This would be facilitated by QR codes in the live game.
  - A digital clue to be delivered by the game's Twitter account
- Placeholder graphics for the "game board" and player avatar
- A database to log player activities (timestamp, record ID, player ID, clue ID, points award)
- Preliminary **PHP** code to connect the activity database with the public game board database accessible via the game's WordPress-based site

This treatment uncovered problems with the game board design, the avatar scale, and some incompatibility with previously written code. But it also helped the team validate the "voice" of the Twitter account, the database schema, and a number of additional assumptions made by the team. We also found that while two game clues were enough to test the game's interaction with the real world, it was not enough to determine if we were meeting our primary learning objective: identification of best practices, opportunities, and potential problems of BYOT programs. This objective would have to be tackled with a larger clue pool later in the production phase.

Building the Components

Once the treatment has been tested and reviewed, the team should document any design changes and update the project schedule before moving on to full production. This might include video production, web site development, creation of social media accounts, and the installation of hardware and software tools.

During this portion of production, it is important to communicate updates weekly and sometimes daily to the entire team. This can be done face-to-face or via digital communication and project management tools. The Google suite of productivity tools (Docs, Sheets, Slides, and Forms) is free and available on a wide array of platforms, making it an excellent choice for keeping the development teams up to date. Additionally, Asana, Smartsheet, and Trello are the top fee-based solutions.

Preparing to Fail

Another component of the production phase is testing. "Fail early" is a favorite mantra for many interactive multimedia teams. Failure is a fact of life when tackling creative endeavors. Not every idea will pan out, and not every approach will work as anticipated. Throughout this phase the development team will continually test assumptions made in the preproduction phase. Is type readable at the specified size? Can users connect to a web application via Wi-Fi? Are points gained by completing activities accurately tallied by the system? Are users motivated to work together? These are the types of questions that should be discussed and debated during the production phase. By testing and failing early the development team can identify potential problems with the content or the digital solutions. Problems identified at this juncture should be addressed either by correcting the issue or by identifying a solution that can be tested during postproduction.

POSTPRODUCTION

Where production is about creating the ARG's content, components, and technologies, postproduction is where those elements are given life. During this phase the development team begins by assembling various elements developed during production. Special consideration is given to how each component will affect the user, and if needed, improvements can be initiated. This is also where the creative teams move from crafting to refining, which can be a difficult transition. With the wide range of possibilities, it is impossible to list all of the activities that might take place during this phase, but here are some common activities:

- Build ARG story websites; live site, post-event site

- Acquire and populate social media accounts

- Regularly conduct functional and integration testing

- Subdivide written and visual content into usable chunks

- Move written, visual, and auditory chunks of content to the online storage system where content will be managed during game play

- Beta test digital integration

- Develop go-live script

- Run complete live test with new users

- Document revisions

GO-LIVE

Before your project goes live, a final round of user experience testing should take place. During this **soft launch**, inexperienced users are given an opportunity to play through all, or as much as is practical, of the game experience. The goal is to put your masterpiece into the hands of people who represent your target audience and, in preparation for going live, to further educate the team on how the audience will approach the game's challenges and activities.

Starting the Game

The direct method for starting your game involves announcing the game's existence and preparing the players. This may require a registration process or simply gathering everyone in one room for the pronouncement. Rabbit hole events, on the other hand, serve as an indirect method for introducing players to the game world.

In either case, ARGs have a go-live date and time. Even those managed by digital systems should indicate a moment when the development team and experienced managers can expect to see traffic indicative of user interaction.

Monitoring the Experience

As the game is underway, technical and creative teams are "on duty" monitoring the game's activities. These individuals are known as *puppet-masters* because they manage the resources and game systems from behind the scenes, unbeknownst to the players and often removed from the environment. Puppet-masters are crucial to running a successful game. Their duties include shepherding actors, analyzing web traffic, answering player emails, monitoring social media channels for inquiries and cheating, checking servers for malicious activities, and policing physical clues. But they can also have more hands-on duties in the role of a game's mole or saboteur.

Some teams also employ **game-masters**. Where puppet-masters are "behind the curtain" serving as allies and adversaries, game-masters are in front of the curtain being a direct line of support to the player. These individuals help the game along by providing direct support to the players. Answering questions face-to-face, making general announcements, settling disputes, and keeping everyone happy are just some of the duties associated with this role.

During *The Pocket* ARG we had several clues posted around the conference hall. These were basic 8.5 × 11 sheets either taped to a wall or in small plastic easels sitting on tables. These sheets were white and printed with codes or odd instructions, which were important to players, but expected to be ignored by non-playing attendees. Day 1 of the event went well. Participants were easily able to find the codes, complete activities, and progress their avatar on the game board. But, overnight some clues went missing and Day 2 started with complaints from many confused players. The on-site game-masters found that the cleaning crew had removed many of the wall-mounted clues, thinking they were remnants of events from Day 1. Luckily within a few minutes of the first complaints, the team was able to print replacement codes and remount them in the conference hall. Once the event was concluded, the team debriefed the incident and it was documented for future ARGs.

Ending the Game

Event-driven ARGs usually have finite start and end dates. As the experience comes to a close, the team monitoring gameplay has the luxury of preparing for a gentle end of game play activities. However, some ARGs are created and released and then take on a life of their own existing well beyond the game's timeline. The game's web sites and physical media are still available to be found by new players to experience.

For the release of their fifth studio album, *Year Zero*,[2] Nine Inch Nails and 42 Entertainment released an ARG that focused on some particular US government policies of 2007. The ARG criticized the government by illustrating how these policies could affect the world of 2022. This was essentially a three-month ARG. The events played out over the time span with players joining in whenever they stumbled across one of the many rabbit hole events.

In some ARGs the end of the game is the start of the analysis phase. Businesses, educational institutions, and training departments use this milestone to start assessing the game's ROI and to start formal analysis of collected data. This information is used to determine the efficacy of the participation activities and the overall success of the project.

DEBRIEF

The goal of a debrief session is to review the team's experience with designing, producing, and executing the ARG. There are many corporate examples of conducting this type of review. Currently we are following a modified version of an "After Action Report" used by the U.S. Air Force. This one- or two-session meeting is meant to discuss outcomes of the ARG. The goal is to improve the production process and reflect on the results of the actual event. The following questions are used to structure the conversation:

1. Evaluate the ARG's goals

    a. What were our intended results?

    b. What were our actual results?

    c. What caused our results?

2. Identify the team's strengths

3. Identify areas of improvement

This discussion is conducted with the entire team in an informal setting, usually involving food. During these meetings participants are asked to refrain from pointing fingers, but instead discuss the issues in terms of what took place, identify opportunities for future improvements, and celebrate the successes. Simply working together on the ARG won't guarantee success on future projects. But, debrief meetings help identify strengths while providing an opportunity to self-correct and enhance individual performance.

Remember that the approach presented here is very general, relying on a merging of common production phases from the entertainment industry (film and stage), of software development (SDLC), and of guidelines for building effective training and performance tools (the ADDIE process). As with most creative endeavors, the success of working with multiple disciplines, roles, approaches, media formats, and technology platforms over a long period of time relies on careful planning, embracing change, and a strong commitment to the project's goals. Before beginning on this development journey, we would suggest visiting the book's companion website, which includes additional case studies, white papers, production tools, and industry techniques: http://www.gamificationforperformance.com.

ENDNOTES

1 ARGology is an effort to aggregate information about alternate reality games—http://bit.ly/4_ARGDesign
2 *Year Zero* was an alternate reality game created by Nine Inch Nails and 42 Entertainment—http://bit.ly/4_YearZero

CHAPTER 5

Storytime

Story and narrative in ARGs have been referred to in various ways throughout the first four chapters. Chapter 1 starts with a story excerpt from an ARG for new student orientation. The chapter then goes on to explain an ARG as being "built around a story that engages the players through an anomaly in their regular daily schedule." In Chapter 2, ideas for ARG scenarios are offered to present the potential for ARGs to meet business goals. Several ARGs are also profiled in Chapter 2, including the description of the story on which the ARG is based. Chapter 3 reviews several ARG profiles, including the premise of each profile. Chapter 4 describes the way in which teams work together to craft the story throughout all phases of the project. An ARG is built around player goals and objectives but is often fueled by the story. The depth and breadth of the story can vary and the importance of the story to the player may vary throughout the ARG experience. But, there's no doubt that the ongoing storyline in the game is what makes ARGs different from other learning and performance improvement formats.

Stories in TV and movies are mainly meant to entertain. An ARG story should be entertaining but also needs to be functional. The story needs to draw the players into the game and create a bridge between non-player characters, media elements, other players, digital activities, and the gameplay that takes place in the real world.

In the *Robots Are Eating the Building* ARG (profiled in Chapter 3), the story of the robots was used to kick off the game during the opening session of the conference. With all the conference attendees in the auditorium, the host directed everyone to a pretend "live" feed from

FIGURE 5.1 Video frame from *Robots Are Eating the Building.*

the security desk (it was a recorded video). The security area was being introduced as a hub for information and directions if attendees needed assistance during the conference. The video showed a standard CCTV security video display with four separate feeds from various parts of the building (see Figure 5.1). As the feed from the security desk was being highlighted and emphasized as a place for information and directions, the other feeds began to go fuzzy and out of focus. Screams were heard in the background. Text replaced the video feeds to proclaim, "Robots Are Eating the Building! Play If You Dare!!!" Med Bot, Mil Bot, Ed Bot, Biz Bot, Consult Bot, and ID Bot were then introduced as the robots eating the building. A URL where conference attendees could register to play was displayed as the final screen of the video.

The story was used to draw the players into the game. It also provided additional context to the cards in the attendee packets that players used to participate in the game. Attendees were given a game card for each of the five robots. These cards included three to five blank fields where information needed to be collected to defeat each robot. (Figure 3.1 shows the Instructional Design Bot.) The robot story also promoted gameplay by providing a theme and overarching goal (defeat the robots and save the building). The story provided a gateway for talking with conference attendees from different industries as part of conference activities. A scavenger hunt without the story would not have been as much fun and would not have resulted in the integrated theme that provided gameplay purpose and motivation.

The story for an ARG should provide direction and context for gameplay. It should address both personal and group goals. The ultimate player reward may be winning the game, winning a prize, or receiving some other sort of recognition. But, the story goal should be about saving the day, discovering a new opportunity, or overcoming adversity, both at an individual and group level. The story ties together the gameplay elements and the interactions between players and non-player characters (NPCs).

The ARG story is not only important for immediate motivation, engagement, and purpose. It's also important for long-term learning and behavior change. Stories connect with our emotions, something that is usually lacking from traditional training, performance change, or employee engagement initiatives. Emotional experiences are memorable experiences.

PLAYER TYPES

In addition, the story presents opportunities to satisfy the different ways in which individual players might interact with the game. There is a well-established player psychology model used to classify players of multiplayer online games called the **Bartle Test of Gamer Psychology**.[1] Created in the late 1990s, the Bartle Quotient calculates a level of preference in each of four categories: **Killer, Socializer, Achiever,** and **Explorer.** Like any psychological profile, an individual is not one "type" versus another, but a combination of types with some types being stronger than others. The Bartle Test reminds us that there are a variety of player types and that the more types the game mechanics and story can address, the more likely it is the game will appeal to a broad audience. At the same time, specific player types can also be targeted through game mechanics and story for specific audiences.

Killers (or Griefers) thrive on extreme competition and prefer player-to-player challenges, versus collaboration in gameplay. This player type likes to have an impact on the game environment by either deconstructing it (yes, blowing it up) or constructing it (building their own personal space). Killers also like to control gameplay through dominating other players via either the game mechanics, **socialsphere**, or **marketplace**. The Killer player type thrives on player-to-player action in the game. The ARG story and game mechanics can address the Killer player type by presenting frequent opportunities for "wins," pitting players against each other, or providing ways to impact the strategy of other players. Player-to-player trivia competitions or single player mini-games, the results of which might allow the ability to reduce or stop other players' progress, are examples of opportunities for "wins" that can be written into the story and game for Killers. The story and game design should also account for Killers' potential disruptive behavior if they get bored.

Socializers like to interact with other players or characters. A game is primarily a social mechanism for them. Rather than achieving a win-state, collecting, or exploring, Socializers play games for the relationships that result from gameplay. Relationships? You can create relationships by playing games? Sure you can. Games can provide player-to-player interactions and player-to-non-player character interactions (quasi-relationships). Many games also involve a community of players (physical and/or digital) that discuss, collaborate, and trash-talk around the gameplay. Like movies and television, players discuss the game's plot, the characters, and what they would do if they were the producer. Video game players also discuss tips-and-tricks, **Easter eggs**, and **cheat codes**. The ARG story should include characters and ways to "interact" with those characters (physically or virtually) for Socializers. The ARG game mechanics should allow player-to-player interactions as part of gameplay or in support of playing the game. There can be opportunities for players to physically gather together as part of the story and game. Or, there can be discussion threads, live chats, web conferencing, and a variety of other opportunities for players to interact in the ARG. The design of social interactions should be purposeful, however. Socializers like to … socialize. Design the social elements of the ARG story and game so that Socializers don't turn the ARG into the company water cooler with a 100% focus on socializing.

Achievers are collectors … of anything and everything.. Points, badges, tools, and levels all represent success in the game to Achievers, whether or not the collection of those items impacts the final outcome of the game to any degree. Achievers are competitive like Killers but are more focused on competing against the game and themselves versus other players. The story's focus on solving a problem or achieving a final goal is important to Achievers. Collection of achievements needs to be balanced with challenge for Achievers. Although the focus of their competitive nature is not on other players, per se, Achievers do like to be recognized as successful in the game. And, extra opportunities that can be presented to Achievers based on their success are also coveted. The ARG story and game mechanics should include a variety of opportunities to achieve success and have that success represented in the game for Achievers. Layers and branches of the story that may only be accessed by those that achieve a certain level or status should also be considered for this player type. Collecting items, solving puzzles, playing trivia games, unlocking clues, and completing levels are game mechanics that appeal to Achievers. And, consider a time-based element to completing tasks with more points given to those that complete the task the quickest. Achievements, recognition titles, scoreboards, and leaderboards round out the Achievers' experience as ways to represent their success in the game to others. Design the story and game so that achieving isn't the only focus, though. And, don't make achieving too easy. Achievers like the success, but they also like the challenge.

Scoreboards and leaderboards can be considered differently. Scoreboards show a player's number score, usually a cumulative score, in relation to other players. A leaderboard can show top performers in sequence, but usually by a designation other than number score. Leaderboards can be cumulative but can also show the most active, most efficient, or most collaborative players for only a segment of gameplay. Example: A scoreboard displays: Player 1 = 2,305 points; Player 2 = 2,065 points; Player 3 = 1,904 points. A leaderboard displays: Player 1 = Level 11 | 3 badges; Player 2 = Level 10 | 5 badges; Player 3 = Level 10 | 2 badges.

Explorers are the fourth and final player type category in the Bartle Quotient. Explorers like to play the game within the game. They like to find hidden treasures, alternate pathways, Easter eggs, and unknown glitches. The backstory of characters, the environment, and the current state are important to Explorers. It gives them context from which to plan their own exploration during gameplay. Variety is important to Explorers. It's the reward for exploring: finding something new or unique. The ARG story and game mechanics should provide opportunities for "wandering" to appeal to Explorers. Consider hidden non-player characters, nondescript resource indicators, and vague innuendos in the story and gameplay to keep Explorers interested. Consider how to keep Explorers on task in the ARG if you have learning and performance objectives throughout. Otherwise, Explorers will find the hidden gems within the game but may not achieve the knowledge, skills, or attitude change that the ARG is targeting.

My Bartle Quotient is Achiever=67%; Killer=60%; Explorer=47%; Socializer=27%, which makes A-K-E-S my player DNA! Goals and rewards are what drive me. But, I also like the adventure and, every so often, some collaboration and interaction with other players does me good. Like most personality tests, the quotient does not define us as one thing versus another. We all have a bit of every personality- or player-type in us. But, there is a dominant way in which each of us approaches life and gameplay.

Take the Bartle Test on the gamificationforperformance.com website and find out what your preferences are for game interactions, defined by your Bartle Quotient.

The consideration of all player types in the design of an ARG and the ARG's story makes it more likely that everyone who plays will enjoy the experience at some level. An audience analysis may also reveal that the targeted players of the ARG at your organization may prefer a certain type of gameplay. For example, one might assume that accountants are Explorers, salespeople are Killers, and nurses could be a combination of Socializers and Explorers. However, it's dangerous to make generalizations. Ultimately, a thoughtful audience analysis is needed to determine whether you want to target specific player types in your story and gameplay or create an ARG experience that will appeal to everyone in some way. A thorough audience analysis, including one done through the lens of the Bartle player types, is recommended before creating the ARG story and game mechanics. Figure 5.2 illustrates the distribution of player types among a group of military leaders in a game design workshop. The Achiever and Killer player types are most prominent (lowest scores), which is to be expected with high-achieving military personnel. Also notice that the Socializer player type is not strongly represented. In this case the evaluation of the audience using the Bartle Quotient leads to less emphasis and prioritization on Socializer story elements and gameplay mechanics when creating an ARG for this group.

A	E
1 3 2 2 2 3 2	3 1 3 3 4 2 3
1 2 4 2 1	2 1 3 3 2
Total 25	Total 30

S	K
4 2 4 4 3 1 4	2 4 1 1 1 4 1
3 4 1 4 3	4 3 2 1 4
Total 37	Total 29

FIGURE 5.2 Audience analysis using the Bartle Quotient.

STORY STRUCTURE

The ARG story can help to create structure as well as change direction in gameplay. The monomyth,[2] or **hero's journey**, is a complex narrative pattern that has been established as the primary way in which stories have been structured from mythology to modern-day movies. There are 8, 12, or 17 stages to the hero's journey depending on which interpretation you choose to use. The stages represent a structure that can also be followed for creating an ARG's story.

Hero's Journey: (1) The Ordinary World, (2) The Call to Adventure, (3) Refusal of the Call, (4) Meeting with the Mentor, (5) Crossing the Threshold, (6) Tests, Allies, and Enemies, (7) Approach, (8) The Ordeal, (9) The Reward, (10) The Road Back, (11) The Resurrection, (12) Return with the Elixir.

In an ARG, the players can be the main character or may play the role of someone who is aiding (or disrupting) the main character. At the beginning of the hero's journey the main character is introduced along with the presence of an underlying conflict. Then, the status quo is disrupted and the main character must consider their role in the change or challenge. In phase three (3) of the hero's journey the main character questions his established role and has to determine whether to turn away from the challenge. Then, the hero encounters a force (a person, skill, or resource) that gives her the ability to face the challenge. At phase five (5) of the hero's journey the main character commits to the adventure and overcoming the challenge. (Phases 6–11 are summarized as follows.) After committing to the journey, the hero is tested, supported by allies, and confronted with enemies. After minor challenges and tests, the hero and his allies are confronted with a significant challenge that they must prepare for. As the story progresses, an ultimate challenge is faced by the hero. Overcoming the ultimate challenge prepares the hero for success during the rest of the journey, even though success is not assured. The hero is strengthened to overcome the final test and resolve the challenge that began the journey. Phase twelve (12) details the hero's transformation from the experience and her journey home or on to another adventure. You have seen the hero's journey played out numerous times in popular film: *The Wizard of Oz*; *The Silence of the Lambs*; *O Brother, Where Art Thou?*; *Star Wars*; *The Matrix*; and *The Lord of the Rings*, just to name a few.

Don't worry. Your ARG story doesn't need to be the next major motion picture blockbuster or great American novel. A well-crafted story can also be considered, more simply, as having a beginning, a middle, and an end, also referred to as the Three Act Structure. The structure of a story can help to establish the need for activities in the game and introduce the initial challenges (beginning), present the main challenge and conflicts (middle), and lead the players to a new state of knowledge, performance, or understanding (end).[3] In the *Robots Are Eating the Building* ARG the need for activity was established with the video introduction described earlier in this chapter (beginning). The main challenge was established and gameplay was encouraged by updates to the robots' statuses and the building's integrity (middle). The storyline was concluded through updates about robots that were defeated and the players who defeated them (end). The *I Love Trees* ARG for the PA Educational Technology Expo & Conference (PETE&C) introduced players to a challenge that was familiar and motivational. And, it was done in a fun and playful way through the Principal Wiggins character (beginning). The main challenge and conflicts were presented through the tree-shaped game board, arbor-related challenges (pests, disease, etc.), Tweets, puzzles, subsequent announcements and appearances from Principal Wiggins, and the public leaderboard (middle). The conclusion was also presented to each player through the completion of the tree-shaped game board, Tweets, a Principal Wiggins announcement, and the leaderboard (end).

If you're looking to create that great blockbuster, be sure to read *Save the Cat!* by Blake Snyder—http://www.amazon.com/Save-Last-Book-Screenwriting-Youll/dp/1932907009

CREATING YOUR ARG STORY

Regardless of whether the ARG is for entertainment and marketing or training and performance improvement, creating the story is a creative endeavor. Like most creative endeavors it can be a messy activity. And, each person will go about it differently. There are a variety of story crafting methods and techniques that are beyond the scope of this book, but here are some considerations for crafting your ARG story.

Start with a Plot, Setting, and Subject

The plot can be very basic to begin with. Start with the beginning (introduce the goal), middle (overcome challenges), and end (realize an altered/

improved state). Later you can build simple and complex interactions (game mechanics) as well as *twists* around the basic story elements. And, remember that an ARG is a live event (digital and/or physical), the direction of which might change based on how players interact with the story and the game. So, leave room in the story for adaptation and plan for adjustments that the puppet-master may need to make throughout the game. Your story plot, setting, and subject can be fictional or realistic and connected or disconnected to your performance improvement goal. If you're creating an ARG to improve the efficiency of meetings in your financial services organization, you may not want to create a story that is based around improving the efficiency of meetings in a financial services organization. You may want to consider a fictional, disconnected story focused on creating more efficient meetings for the League of Justice (go figure, Superman is never on time for meetings). Or you might consider a realistic, disconnected story focused on creating more efficient meetings for the local parent-teacher organization. Consider the variety of plot, setting, subject, and gameplay options for an ARG story with the combination of Realistic|Connected, Realistic|Disconnected, Fictional|Connected, or Fictional|Disconnected points of view. Pick one from column A and one from column B in Table 5.1 to begin crafting your story.

There are a number of story creator sites and apps that can help you generate ideas for your story if there aren't any apparent storylines for you to follow. Brainstormer[4] is one story creator that we've used. While the tool normally doesn't spit out *the* story plot, setting, and subject for

TABLE 5.1   Story Perspectives

Column A		Column B	
Realistic	The story and/or the player's role is realistic. Realism helps to connect the game to work/life, puts the player in a role they will play in the real world, and creates a recognizable context for learning	Connected	A connected perspective is one in which the challenges, actions, and decisions are explicitly connected to the performance goals for the player.
Fictional	The story and/or the player's role is fictional. Fiction can aid immersion and increase the fun factor. Fiction can also support *game balance*.	Disconnected	A disconnected perspective is one in which the challenges, actions, and decisions are implicitly connected to the performance goals for the player.

your story, it does help to get the creative story crafting juices flowing. The following are some examples of Brainstormer-generated plot, setting, and subject combinations:

Letting Go → Attic → B-Movie

Fish Out of Water → Chef → Eskimo

Odd Couple → Inventor's Lab → Stuffy British

Remorse → Ninja → Steampunk

Create Characters

There are very rarely "*player characters*" in an ARG; players "play" as themselves as opposed to taking on the role of an established protagonist. There may be an opportunity for players to represent themselves with an avatar or a unique screen name, but in most ARGs the players don't play a character role in the story or the gameplay. I emphasize the lack of player characters in "most ARGs." But, just because it isn't a common approach doesn't mean it can't be done. That's the great thing about ARGs. There's not one, precise formula for creating an alternate reality game. NPCs, the characters not controlled by players, can play any number of roles in the ARG story and gameplay. Table 5.2 describes the impact NPCs can have in an ARG.

When you think of characters for your ARG, go beyond creating only human-like representations. Characters can be fictional people. But, objects and places can also be non-player characters in the game. Regardless of the form of the character or the purpose for the character, there are a variety of *character types*[5] to consider as you craft your ARG story and build your character elements.

The *hero character* is the player character in most games. An avatar represents the player character as a hero who plays to overcome a problem and transform himself, herself, or itself and the world in which the hero lives. In an ARG the hero can be a non-player character and the ARG player can be a director, supporter, or observer of the hero's journey. Or, the ARG player may undertake the activities of the hero, but not as a specific character. Remember, players in an ARG usually play as themselves.

The *shadow character* represents the hero's opposite: an adversary who is assumed as responsible for the hero's problems. The revealing of the shadow in the story can be a twist, revealed as the dark side of the

TABLE 5.2   Examples of Using Non-Player Characters in an ARG

Introduce the rabbit hole	The rabbit hole is the hook into the game. A non-player character can be used to make players aware of the game and initiate gameplay.
Establish the objective	A character can establish the reason for playing the ARG. Think M from the James Bond films, or Charlie from *Charlie's Angels*. An NPC can deliver an urgent message to establish the overall goal of playing the game. Or, a character can recur throughout the game to provide incremental objectives for gameplay.
Provide information	Characters might play a large role in the story and gameplay and appear every time a clue is given, puzzles are solved, or information is requested. A character may also appear at crucial moments of gameplay to encourage players to complete a task that will establish expectations or build momentum.
Guide players	A non-player character can be available as a guide throughout the game, giving hints and advice to guide players to success. The guide can be automatically presented to players or the players may have to request guidance from the character.
Distract players	Contrary to a guide, a character can be used to distract players with misinformation or require players to complete an additional task to get around an obstacle the non-player character presents.
Reinforce the storyline	The story is interwoven with gameplay in an ARG, but sometimes the specifics of gameplay activities become a greater emphasis at the expense of the story. Characters can be used to bring players back into the story and reestablish motives, emotional connections, and fun.
Adjust the storyline and gameplay	As mentioned previously throughout this book, the ARG story and gameplay may need to be adjusted by the puppet-master. Characters can be a part of the change in direction and communicating the new direction to players.
Conclude gameplay	Just as a character can be useful for starting an ARG, an NPC can be used to summarize gameplay and let players know that they've reached the end.

hero, a former friend of the hero, or just someone or something in the story that's an unexpected shadow. A shadow character might be used to introduce the rabbit hole, distract ARG players, reinforce the storyline, or adjust the storyline and gameplay.

The *mentor character* often guides the ARG player toward some action, prepares the player for the journey, and guides the player throughout gameplay. The mentor may be someone who has taken the same journey as the player is undertaking and provides wisdom based on her previous success or failure. The mentor character might be used for any character role in the ARG outlined in Table 5.2.

Ally characters help the ARG player progress throughout the game. Allies may also help the player get past obstacles that are too difficult to overcome by himself. An ally character can be used for any character roles in the game outlined in Table 5.2. But an ally can also be another real-world player of the game working on the same challenges as the player

Guardian characters present an obstacle to the ARG player in her journey until she has proven her worth. A guardian character might require a feat of strength, intelligence, or compassion before providing the information or path that the player needs to continue. A guardian character can be used to provide information, distract players, reinforce the storyline, or adjust the storyline and gameplay in the ARG.

Trickster characters cause chaos through their pranks and foolishness. Tricksters mainly play neutral roles in the story and may just be used as a form of comic relief or to provide a transition in the story from one stage to another. A trickster character can be used to introduce the rabbit hole, distract players, or adjust the storyline and gameplay in the ARG.

Herald characters bring a message to the player that generates action, emotional change, or movement in a new direction. A herald character can be used to introduce the rabbit hole, establish the objective, guide players, reinforce the storyline, or adjust the storyline and gameplay in the ARG.

There are a number of character description templates available online that help to outline the main characteristics of a character as well as character bible templates that guide the establishment of a much more detailed character description and history. Search on "character description template" or "character bible" for a wealth of resources.

Like story creator software and sites, there are character creator resources as well. The Brainstormer app also includes a Character Builder option (for an additional $.99). The character builder add-on "mixes personalities, backgrounds, and themes for an unending variety of compelling characters." The character example provided with the Character Builder option in Brainstormer is "The Self-made Man/Genius/Naturalist."

Consider the Physical Space

ARGs take place in the real world and the best ARGs take advantage of the physical space in which the game is being played. In addition to digital activities like Tweeting, web-based games, and digital codes, players may have to visit specific physical locations for gameplay, communication, or collaboration. The physical space can also play a role in the story. In the *Find the Future* ARG, the New York Public Library's flagship building was the story. In the *Robots Are Eating the Building* ARG, the story of the potential "destruction" of the space where the conference participants were attending sessions, eating lunch, and networking introduced tension, motivation, and humor to the story. Consider how the space in which participants are playing can be used to support and enhance the story and gameplay.

Consider the Timeline

The ARG story needs to have a beginning, a middle, and an end that occurs along a story timeline. But, the ARG will also have a real-time timeline. Consider the number of days, weeks, months, or years that it will take players to complete the ARG. A longer ARG timeline may require a more elaborate ARG story and deeper character development. A shorter ARG can be supported by a simpler story. In fact, it's important that a one-, two-, or three-day ARG have a simple story. When there is only a short amount of time for players to complete the ARG gameplay, an elaborate story can get in the way of players completing tasks in the game. They will spend more time trying to determine and understand the motivation and objectives defined in the story than completing gameplay and achieving learning and performance objectives.

Create the Rabbit Hole

As described throughout this book, the rabbit hole is the entry into the ARG for the players. It may be explicit and easily discovered and accessed. An example of an explicit rabbit hole is an email sent to all new hires asking them to watch a video from the president of the company that describes the story, gameplay, and expectations of players. Or, the rabbit hole can be implicit and disguised within the everyday environment of the potential player. An example of an implicit rabbit hole is an anonymous Post-it note left on each new hire's desk announcing a meeting in the conference room at 1 p.m. As noted in Chapter 2, ARGs for business often require 100% participation. So, an explicit rabbit hole is preferred for onboarding, training, and performance improvement ARGs. So, while the rabbit hole event introduces the player to the gamplay, it can also provide a glimpse of the plot, theme, or characters within the story.

Create a Backstory

The ARG backstory can serve several purposes. Depending on how you introduce the rabbit hole, the backstory can provide a prelude to the rabbit hole, giving players some context regarding how the current state came to be when they enter the game. The backstory can also be a way to address the interests of players who are primarily the Explorer player-type. Remember that the backstory of characters, the environment, and the current state are important to Explorers. It gives them context from which to plan their own exploration during gameplay. The backstory can also be a source of interest for Achievers as well. As Explorers and Achievers review the backstory there can be opportunities to find hidden treasures and/or gateways to move forward in the game without having to take the normal path.

Tell the Story across Multiple Mediums

ARGs are **transmedia storytelling**. Take advantage of the opportunity that multiple mediums present. Tell the story on paper, with sidewalk chalk, and with signs. Tell the story with video, graphics, and animation. Tell the story with Twitter, Facebook, LinkedIn, SharePoint, and Pinterest. It's not an ARG if there aren't multiple forms and formats as the player experiences and participates in the story.

Incorporate Collaborative Storytelling

A well-designed ARG provides opportunities for players to interact with and even impact the story individually, in groups, or based on cumulative play (see *Find the Future* in Chapter 2). Consequently, the puppet-master, who observes the overall gameplay, must be available to make edits or create additions to the story and gameplay based on the cumulative actions being observed. Opportunities for players to impact the story through individual or group gameplay should be identified and taken advantage of. Observation of gameplay and subsequent changes to story and interactions should also be considered when creating the initial ARG story.

Simple Is Better Than Complex

Story writing has been presented in an orderly fashion here. In actuality, it's anything but orderly. You may write the end of your story before you write the beginning. You might create characters first and then a theme and plot. Regardless of your order, interactive story writing is an iterative process that will go through numerous stages and drafts before it's logical, playable, and entertaining. Remember that an ARG story should be entertaining, but it also needs to be functional.

The story should not be too complex. Err on the side of simplicity for an ARG that is focused on improving knowledge, skills, and attitudes. A complex story can confuse players and bring the gameplay to a halt. When players are participating in the ARG as part of their job, they need to balance ARG gameplay with getting their work done and balancing their lives. Also remember that you're most likely targeting 100% audience participation in an ARG for business. A complex story can turn players off right from the very beginning and jeopardize reaching 100% participation. A complex story can also jeopardize completion within the targeted timeframe. If it takes players a few hours in a daylong ARG to understand the story and what they should be doing, it's likely they'll be rushing through (or skipping) later gameplay elements in order to complete the gameplay on time.

The story and gameplay should be intertwined. It seems reasonable, but creating game mechanics that are linked to learning objectives and support a storyline can be complex. It's easy to lose sight of the story and characters as you focus on incorporating learning objectives, practice activities, and learning collaboration into the game. At the same time, it's easy to lose track of the performance objectives as the creative juices begin flowing and you get immersed in writing a story and developing characters. As is the challenge with most serious games and immersive learning, ARGs for business and training need to have an effective mix of learning-focus and fun-focus. If there's too much focus on learning and performance objectives, the ARG won't be fun and it won't be much different than other boring training sessions. If there's too much focus on fun, the players won't learn anything and there won't be any positive impact on employee or business performance.

ENDNOTES

[1] The Bartle Test of Gamer Psychology—http://bit.ly/5_Bartle

[2] The hero's journey is a common narrative pattern—http://bit.ly/5_Hero

[3] Why You Need to Use Storytelling for Learning—http://bit.ly/5_Storytelling

[4] The Brainstormer 2.0 is a tool for randomly generating a plot, subject, and setting—http://bit.ly/5_Brainstorm1

[5] *Game Development Essentials*, Jeannie Novak, 2nd edition

CHAPTER 6

10 Participation Points for Gryffindor

So far we've discussed what an ARG is, how it can be used for learning and collaboration, the development process, and the importance of story. In this chapter we'll focus on answering, "How will the player interact with the game world?" This will generally be a discussion on marrying the story with various technologies, but we will first look at motivating participation.

Almost any type of media can be integrated into a technology platform. Platforms can be as simple as pen and paper or as complex as fully featured virtual worlds spanning multiple devices, languages, and input types. The decision regarding which technologies and platforms are right for you depends on a number of variables, most notably the player's participation.

AVOID TECHNOLOGY DISTRACTIONS

During gameplay, players could be rushing between physical locations, scouring libraries and websites, or collaborating on crucial clues about non-player characters (NPC) and the backstory. Because of these varying activities, you'll need to design player interactions to be short, targeted, and self-explanatory. This approach is designed to keep the player "in the game world," living the story events in real-time toward the game's goals and objectives. Nothing will kill player motivation faster than being ripped from the story to load third-party plugins, deal with an incompatible mobile device, hunt down a reliable Wi-Fi connection, or stumble over other unnecessary technology hurdles.

MAKE A PLAN

The first task to determining a technology platform is identifying player interactions. Before slapping on a collection of technology solutions because they're familiar or easy to acquire, it's important to fully understand three things about the player and the story: (1) the types of interactions the player will have within the story world, (2) the frequency of those interactions, and (3) the resources and expertise needed to implement the platform(s). We address these questions during the preproduction phase using a tool from traditional storytelling—the **beat sheet**.

Novelists and screenwriters use beat sheets to sequence activities taking place in a story or script. In ARG development, we similarly use the beat sheet to sequence and analyze the player's activities. Figure 6.1 is a portion of a beat sheet created in Microsoft Excel. This example represents an ARG for a new employee orientation program with the goal of increasing employee engagement, introducing company culture, presenting the code of conduct, optimizing training time, and reinforcing new skills. This story-driven, game-based approach sparks engagement and innovation more than the traditional "death by PowerPoint" approach used by many training professionals.

This sequence of activities represents part 2 of an ARG where players are trying to secure a "secret formula" before it falls into the wrong

Beat		Details
2	Start of Part 2	Player receives web link (video message) from Lilia Scott.
2.1	Player discovers combination to safe	Combination is the last four digits of the customer support phone line. Player can retrieve code from company website (About>Contact)
2.2	Player uses combination to open safe	Acquired combination is sent via text or entered into game dashboard. If successful "secret formula" is added to player inventory
2.3	Player returns to Dr. Tovel's Lab with formula	Player returns to Lab to deliver formula.
2.4	Player learns of double-cross	Cari the front desk manager overheard and recorded portions of the mysterious conversation.

FIGURE 6.1   Initial beat sheet example.

hands. It covers privacy policies, state and federal regulations, accessing the company's intranet, and safely navigating around the facility using a spy/mystery theme. Note that each "beat" is numbered for organization and to facilitate referencing specific activities in future beats and revisions.

EVALUATE PLAYER ACTIVITIES

The next step is to evaluate the types of activities associated with each beat of the story. These activities are the means by which players will engage in the story. They describe varying actions and tasks designed to help achieve the ARG's learning and entertainment goals. Some of these activities are passive in nature, like reading, watching, and collecting. These engage the player in simple "viewing" or "information gathering" activities, which can be effective for establishing an emotional mood, presenting new information, or demonstrating a skill. An example of *passive participation* can be seen in the *I Love Trees* ARG. During the registration process, players watched an introductory video from their boss, "Principal Wiggins." The video was instrumental in establishing the player's role in the game, introducing gameplay (identifying resource categories needed for collection), and illustrating how clues were used to advance their individual story. Each of these skills was crucial to playing the game and best delivered through a passive experience.

Some interactions are more active, requiring a higher level of engagement. These are activities where players must make and act upon decisions according to game prompts or NPC requests. Activities like solving puzzles, answering short questions, or completing skill-based tasks are all good examples of active interactions. These actions require increased participation with the world's characters and other physical players. At this level, players are engaging with the world, but they are not involved in creating content or altering the game world. In *Cosmic Voyage Enterprises* from Doubletake Studios and Transmedia Storyteller Ltd., players form into teams of five C-level executive roles (CEO/COO/CMO/CFO/GC). Each group (company) is challenged to address a business problem where each teammate has access to unique information pertinent to their role. The ARG teaches ethics and financial responsibility while requiring team members to collaborate on how their company would respond to the game's social, environmental, and financial challenges. As you can imagine, the players are expected to be highly active in this ARG, moving well beyond passive engagement.

There are also immersive activities. These require the player to connect directly with other participants of the game to advance the shared story. Players might collaborate en masse or form ad hoc teams to utilize role-based skills or craft unique story elements and content. Because of its high level of technical engagement, this is the least common type of participation, but it can create a very rewarding experience. In Jane McGonigal's *World Without Oil*, players are presented with the real-world problem of oil dependency and are asked to document how their lives would be affected by the threat of a global oil shortage. Through blog posts, video diaries, web comics, photographs, and audio clips, players around the world shared unique stories imagining how the shared social and economic turmoil would impact their daily lives. The result is a rich tapestry of stories and imagery that tell the tale of a world plunged into chaos as this natural resource becomes scarce. The game world was alive because of the high level of player participation. Table 6.1 summarizes the levels of participation in ARG activities and the resulting user experience and engagement.

Now that we have an understanding of how players can interact within an ARG, we can go back and take another look at the beat sheet. The original excerpt (Figure 6.1) identifies points in the story where players

TABLE 6.1 Levels of Player Participation and ARG Activities

Participation	Activities	Engagement Examples
Passive	Reading, watching, collecting	• Watching on- or off-line videos to complete a challenge • Reading page 12 of the sales manual • Scanning six QR codes to reactivate a dormant Heim hyperdrive, opening a wormhole back to earth
Active	Puzzles, short challenge questions, light research or collaboration, two-way digital communication	• Completing a cryptogram to unlock the courier's briefcase • Helping Carlos, a virtual sales rep, complete next quarter's sales objectives by analyzing historical data • Tracking down a trainee (another game participant) who has the role of farmer to convert your seeds into crops
Immersive	World building and customization, asset crafting, extensive communication	• Gathering into teams of four to build an ultimate Scooby Doo team (brains, intellect, cunning, and guile) to save Old Man Johnson's dilapidated amusement park.

Beat		Details	Activity	Type
2	Start of Part 2	Player receives web link (video message) from Lilia Scott.	Watch video	P
2.1	Player discovers combination to safe	Combination is the last four digits of the customer support phone line. Player can retrieve code from company website (About>Contact)	Find information	A
2.2	Player uses combination to open safe	Acquired combination is sent via text or entered into game dashboard. If successful "secret formula" is added to player inventory	Enter information	A
2.3	Player returns to Dr. Tovel's Lab with formula	Player returns to Lab to deliver formula.	Move to physical location	A
2.4	Player learns of double-cross	Cari the front desk manager overheard and recorded portions of the mysterious conversation.	Ask questions	A

FIGURE 6.2   Beat sheet including activities and types.

engage with story elements. Figure 6.2 expands the beat sheet by adding the Activity and Participation Type columns further describing the activities associated with each beat. The *P*, *A*, and *I* classifications correspond to the Passive, Active, and Immersive participation levels identified in the previous chart.

With this portion of the beat sheet completed we can take a closer look at identifying technologies to support these activity types. Remember your ARG should inspire, motivate, and engage your audience while the supporting technologies should create minimal friction between the ARG's narrative and the player's input.

After identifying the various activities, it is also good practice to create a summary of activity types. This task will help to understand how well the game's story, activities, feedback, and rewards are balanced for the user (game balance). Additionally, it will provide insight into the number of activities that need to be supported by the technology platforms. Creating a simple bar or pie chart will help visualize the activities in total and can be instrumental in evaluating potential technology solutions.

IDENTIFY TECHNOLOGIES BASED ON PARTICIPATION

The next step is to identify possible technology solutions for each activity type listed on the beat sheet. Since the activities for each ARG are unique, we'll identify some common technologies and how they can be integrated for physical and digital implementations.

Passive Participation

Passive activities are the most basic interactions players will have with the game world. These entail actions such as reading passages, watching video clips, viewing images, or listening to recorded messages. Because of their passive nature and accessibility, we see these activities both incorporated into physical items and hosted through online services.

Passive—physical.

Print materials are the most common usages for passive activities. Clues or messages are presented on business cards, posters, fake newspapers, and handouts. We also see the use of temporary media such as whiteboards, for team tracking, scoring, and notification. But don't rely on these alone; there are also more clever usages of physical print materials such as billboards, T-shirts, skywriting, and QR codes.

Passive—digital.

There are a number of tools available to facilitate digital content for use in passive activities, with standard websites being the primary choice. These sites often have high production value because they typically serve as a player's first point of contact with the game world. At this first point of contact, participants might not realize they are playing a game, and as such, the website has all the appearances of being live, complete with blog entries, active forums, detailed history, and about sections.

But building a full website isn't the only approach. Sometimes the development team just needs to host videos, images, or audio files for players to access. Image and video services like YouTube, Vimeo, Flickr, Instagram, and even Vine allow for sharing content that can be easily accessed, updated, and managed by URL or RSS feed. Adding a URL-shortening service tool like bit.ly will not only shorten the content URL but also mask the host site and create basic web analytics for future analysis.

Lastly **micro-blogging** services like Twitter, Facebook, Google+, Instagram, or simple email messages can be utilized to communicate with players, driving the story and gameplay forward.

In 2007, attendees of the San Diego Comic-Con were introduced to the *Dark Knight* ARG with two passive rabbit hole events. The first was finding one of the mysterious "Jokerized" one-dollar bills, which contained the whysoserious.com URL. This website contained advertisements for the player to join the game as one of Joker's henchmen. The second rabbit hole was a phone number written in the sky; when the number was called, the player heard a message from a whimpering man reading instructions to begin the scavenger hunt portion of the game. The activities, although very passive, show how mixing the physical and game worlds can create rich and rewarding experiences.

Active Participation

Where passive activities deliver information to the player, active participation requires the player to engage with the world through simple tasks. Tasks such as problem solving, acting upon new information (such as those found through passive participation), research, and collaboration are the most common choices.

Active—physical.

Getting the player more involved in the ARG means crafting activities that bridge the game world with the real world. Sometimes this can be as simple as physical movement. Getting players to move from place to place ties individual activities to specific locations. It's common when simulating business or retail activities to have participants move throughout a real-world space simulating the activities tied to the ARG's goals. Retail planners might visit store locations to mine game resources while managing stock levels. Or, new employees might have to scavenge for puzzle pieces as they learn to safely navigate a factory floor while gaining a deeper understanding of OSHA laws and regulations.

Additionally, moving through the game world helps pacing and staging of events. Knowing how many players have made it to a particular location can help the game- and puppet-masters tweak the experience. If a number of players have missed an important location by a designated time, additional clues can be provided to help get players caught up and back on track.

Puzzles and ciphers are another type of physical activity common to ARGs. Simple word puzzles or riddles are often used to challenge individual or group players, but intricate cryptograms, advanced ciphers, or **slow-scan television** images encoded as audio files are also part of this category. Visit http://bit.ly/6_Cipher for more information on these types of challenges.

Active—digital.

As we've seen, websites can deliver information to create a passive user experience, but they can also host active challenges. When combined with server-side scripting languages, websites can deliver dynamic content based on a variety of common variables: username/login (who is the player), access location (where is the player), IP address (what device is the player using), and date/time (when did the interaction occur), to name a few. But a variety of web-based services are also available to provide content and challenges for ARG participants.

In *The Pocket* game, players, who were educators attending PETE&C in early 2012, were put in the role of a school district decision maker. The game used a simple content management system (CMS) website as the primary interaction device. Five hundred thirty-two participants registered at the site to begin play after responding to a cryptic Twitter message and an animated video posted on the conference's social media site. The game was designed to illustrate the usefulness of liberal "bring your own device" policies. Players responded to physical (QR codes and cryptograms) and electronic (#petec12 hashtag) challenges by entering their answers in the website. Aside from a leaderboard, the site also plotted the user's progress on a game board. This progression tool was used to set the player's expectations over the two-day conference by illustrating how many of the 33 clues they had uncovered.

Some of the more innovative solutions come from ARGs built around television programs. *Mr. Robot* debuted in June of 2015 on the USA network. The series is about a cyber-security engineer who is recruited by a mysterious underground group to publicly and financially destroy his employer. As part of the show's promotion, the whoismrrobot.com site hosted a Twitch channel. At the end of the premiere episode, just before the closing commercial break, a mysterious character announces that you can "Get back what is rightfully yours at www.whoismrrobot.com" while displaying a six-character alphanumeric code on the screen.

Viewers who visit the site and enter the code are entered into a live giveaway of $50, $100, or $400. This additional experience wasn't a simple web form, which is often used in these cases; instead it was a live 13-minute broadcast bordering on performance art. The broadcast hosted masked actors interacting with the viewers via chat and a massively multiplayer online role-playing game (MMORG) extending the experience beyond the episode into a quasi-alternate existence. In this case the show posed as the rabbit hole event, inviting viewers to learn more about the show's premise and compete for prizes.

Immersive Participation

As ARGs and interactive storytelling have matured in sophistication and technical support, we have seen the industry move beyond passive and active participation into an area of true immersion. Today there are games that evolve through gameplay; as players immerse themselves in gameplay their actions build a unique world unto itself. ARGs like *World Without Oil* fit into this category because the "game" requires participants to create images, stories, and videos illustrating their interpretation of the future.

Some games are also further blurring the lines between fiction and reality. In the following ARG descriptions you'll read how the designers built a skeletal story but the players brought it to life with content and/or inquiry.

Find the Future.
In the late spring of 2011, 500 people gathered in the Main Hall of the New York Public Library to coauthor a book. These participants were selected from 5,000 online entries where they were asked to demonstrate their creativity by answering the question, "How do you want to make history and change the world?" Once the game began, players chose their group and began what amounted to a building-wide quest for artifacts. Over the course of a single evening, players scoured the library in search of 100 artifacts emblazoned with a QR code. These codes would unlock writing prompts for the team's writers who would then set about providing some fictitious literature about the artifact. The resulting 600+-page book *100 Ways to Make History* is currently on display in the library's rare book section.

Read more about this event from the following first-person articles:

- Big Fuel—http://bit.ly/6_bigfuel

- Brian Fiore-Silfvast—http://bit.ly/6_Silfvast

The Black Watchmen.
This ARG is a more recent example of immersive participation. In *The Black Watchmen* you play as a new recruit in a "paramilitary group dedicated to protecting the public from dangerous phenomena beyond human understanding." On its surface the game plays like many other ARGs except that all communication with the game world happens within an application through a dashboard called the Mission Hub. During the registration phase players can self-select their immersion level. The game offers four color-coded levels, shown in Figure 6.3.

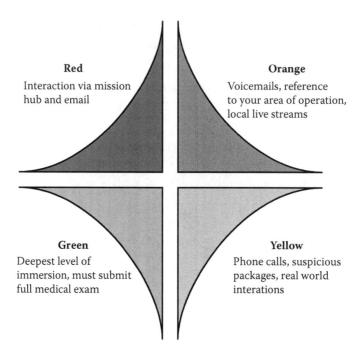

Red
Interaction via mission
hub and email

Orange
Voicemails, reference
to your area of operation,
local live streams

Green
Deepest level of
immersion, must submit
full medical exam

Yellow
Phone calls, suspicious
packages, real world
interations

FIGURE 6.3 *The Black Watchmen* levels of immersion.

In these examples, the ARG itself serves as a vehicle for creation. It's easy to identify how theme, story, and participation go hand in hand. While most of today's business and training ARGs fall in the passive and active participation areas, we expect the technical innovations used in immersive systems to find their way into workplace ARGs very soon.

CREATING SPECIFIC INTERACTIONS

As humans, we enjoy being challenged. More precisely, we gain personal enjoyment from the creative process found in problem solving. We derive joy and satisfaction from completing challenging tasks, especially when competition is involved even if that competition is internal. In the book *Creativity: Flow and the Psychology of Discovery and Invention*, noted researcher and professor of psychology **Mihály Csíkszentmihályi** discusses how we derive enjoyment from the creative process. His research highlights that designing and discovering new things is a common source of happiness. Many of his insights into happiness come from interviews on the subject of personal motivation and how the quality of an experience influences happiness.

From Csíkszentmihályi's interviews, the following nine key elements[1] are most commonly used when describing enjoyable experiences:

1. There are clear goals every step of the way.

2. There is immediate feedback to one's actions.

3. There is a balance between challenges and skills.

4. Actions and awareness are merged.

5. Distractions are excluded from consciousness.

6. There is no worry of failure.

7. Self-consciousness disappears.

8. The sense of time becomes distorted.

9. The activity becomes an end in itself.

Although Csíkszentmihályi used these elements to discuss happiness during the creative process, we often use them as guideposts when developing engaging experiences like ARGs. We loosely assess the tools and decisions around how well they fit into this list, particularly when addressing puzzles, platforms, and social media tools.

Puzzles

Mystery sits at the heart of most ARGs. It arouses curiosity in players and provides a vehicle for thinking critically about the story. In the game world mystery manifests itself through story and puzzles. While mysterious story elements draw players into the game, puzzles promote deeper thinking, coaxing players from passive to active participation. But creating puzzles can be tricky. You want to create a zone of mental focus in which the player is fully immersed in the activity, while straddling the line between anxiety and boredom. This balanced experience represents the Flow Channel,[2] also from Csíkszentmihályi, and is best illustrated as the channel between increasing challenges and player skill. (See Figure 6.4.)

This image depicts the optimal zone in which your player will be engaged. Your puzzles, like many other creative activities, should challenge

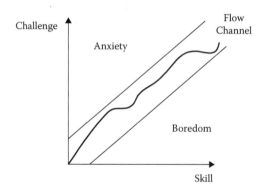

FIGURE 6.4 "Flow" concept by Csíkszentmihályi. Drawn by Senia Maymin.

players by building on previously acquired skills. The pattern in video games usually looks like this:

- Player acquires new skill (e.g., ability, knowledge, artifact, weapon).

- Player engages in low-level activities that require usage of this skill (brief tutorial introducing application of skill).

- Game activities present themselves, which force player to hone the skill (skill-based challenges rendering areas and NPCs inaccessible).

- Player is presented with more complex challenge, which usually requires multiple tries (e.g., boss battles, end-of-level challenges).

- Player proceeds in game world with mastery of the new skill.

These micro-challenges and activities are designed to promote longer-term engagement by alternating gameplay activities between periods of struggle (gaining mastery) and relaxation (applying mastery, successful accomplishment).

In ARGs we use puzzles the same way. Puzzles create small hurdles for the player and opportunities for accomplishment. They serve as gatekeepers to the next phase of the story. They also meet a number of Csíkszentmihályi's key elements: notably numbers 1, 2, 4, 5, 6, and 9.

The Internet is full of design techniques and approaches for creating puzzles. One of the best resources is Adam Foster's aptly named "How to Build Fictionally Appropriate ARG Puzzles That People Have Fun Solving, and Which People Can Solve."[3] In it he discusses using real-world **encoding systems** (QR codes, barcodes, **MD5**, slow-scan television, and

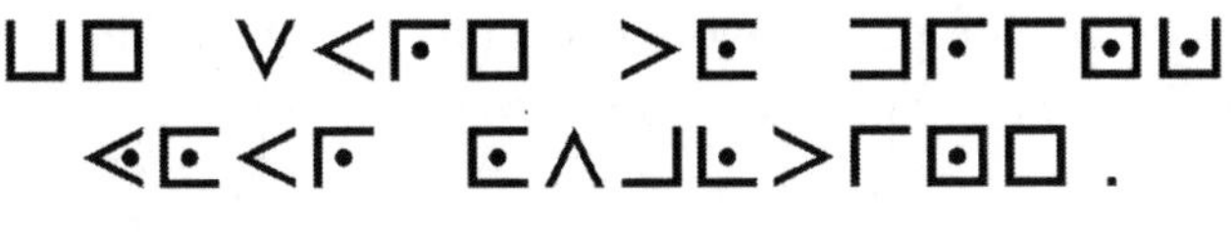

⊔◻ ∨<Γ◻ >ᴄ ⊐ſ·Γ◽⊔
<ᴄ<ſ ᴄ∧⊐Ŀ>Γ◽◻ .

FIGURE 6.5   Pigpen cipher using the BabelStone font.

other cryptographic hashes), avoiding expert-level domain knowledge, false clues, and coincidences. This is an excellent introduction to using encoders to hide information.

Another common puzzle technique is the use of ciphers. Ciphers are simple text manipulation tools used to scramble and unscramble messages. Julius Caesar famously used substitution ciphers to issue commands to military troops.

Using the Caesarian Shift cipher

U'xx yqqf kag uz yk arruoq mf 3:30by.

would be decoded as

I'll meet you in my office at 3:30pm.

For more information on ciphers and **cryptography**, the art of encrypting and decrypting messages, check out the "Journey into Cryptography"[4] course on Khan Academy. But if you just want to jump right in and create a cipher right away, visit Tyler Akins' Rumkin.com site—http://bit.ly/6_Cipher—for a collection of cipher tools and resources. (See the example in Figure 6.5.)

Platforms

Many of today's ARGs use web-based systems to deliver their content. A ubiquitous web platform can support hundreds of players, in multiple locations using an assortment of devices. This means developers can design and deploy a single, commonly accessible delivery system with a high degree of assurance that the end user can receive the message. Although there is no standard system in place, many ARGs use blogging platforms or content management systems[5] (CMS) to achieve this purpose. Among these platforms, WordPress is one of the most common tools.

Content management systems are computer applications that allow for the creation, modification, organization, and publishing of content from a central interface. Their popularity has grown over the years because of their ability to dynamically deliver content, separate editor and programmer roles, simplify deployment, and provide a customizable code base. In our work, we've used WordPress to facilitate story delivery, collect and validate user answers, present leaderboards, visualize puzzles, and display player progress.

Once installed, the CMS can be configured to selectively release content based on time or user activity, or content can be released manually by a puppet-master. Puzzles and story elements appear dynamically as players interact with the site, providing a level of interaction and feedback that can be difficult to maintain with on-site game- and puppet-masters.

Aside from managing player participation in the game world, the CMS can also facilitate group communications. The platform allows for the creation of teams (either predetermined or ad hoc), with content areas such as wikis or forums for teams to share information, puzzle status, notes, or other updates as needed. Although easy to install, an understanding of PHP, MySQL, and Apache is required to customize a CMS system for ARG usage.

A typical CMS solution can also be used to address numbers 2, 4, and 9 from Csíkszentmihályi's key elements of enjoyment.

Aside from a full-blown CMS, any blogging platform or direct messaging system can be used to manage player participation. With instant messaging services like Google Talk, Jabber, or Spark, a single person behind the scenes can provide instant feedback to players in the field, creating a real-time system where NPCs can uniquely react to player activities in ways that other "canned" experiences can't.

Competition

Competition is another tool to engage ARG players. Done properly, competition devices like leaderboards, progress bars, badges/achievements, and rewards (physical or virtual) can empower the four Bartle player types in different fashions. We often think of Killers and Achievers using competition (via status) as a means of validating their performance against others. But Explorers and Socializers also compete for standing in their networks, and devices like leaderboards and achievements provide them with this type of recognition.

Leaderboards are generally associated with point systems. As players complete puzzles or game challenges, they are awarded points. These points, and sometimes levels, are then used to set status within the game. The

LEADERBOARD			Points 5 day total	24hr Streak
15	◊	Paula Batiste	143	-2 ▼
16	❄	Kelli Snyder	136	+5 ▲
17	◊	Glenn McGuigan	128	0 —

FIGURE 6.6   Contextual ranking. This sample identifies the current user, relative ranking, team assignment, and five-day score totals.

leaderboard is one of many devices used to rank player activities. Consider the following devices when integrating competition into your game.

- Contextual ranking: Ranked leaderboards often highlight the top 5 or 10 players. But statistically speaking, most of your players will fall well below this threshold. Kelli Snyder, who currently holds the 16th place in Figure 6.6, is more concerned with incremental successes (overtaking Paula Batiste's 15th slot) than she is with breaking into the top 5. Contextual rankings are used to augment the top player rankings by comparing the player to those closer in point score or level. Often this will be the two players directly above and below in ranking. (See Figure 6.6.)

- Multiple rankings: This device creates multiple categories for ranking. Separate lists for overall scoring, marked improvement, timeframes (e.g., this week, this month, last month), and subgroups (e.g., sales team, facilities management, customer service) provide multiple opportunities for players to be acknowledged.

- Progress bar: Used to keep track of individual goals, the progress bar is an intrinsic motivator letting players compete against themselves.

Point systems can be associated with individual players or teams depending on the nature of the challenge and the purpose of the ARG.

Progress bars and dashboards can be used to help direct players to important tasks or the level of completion of the current tasks. Progress bars illustrate a linear measure of completion, usually depicted by a bar that is partially filled with a highlight color to indicate progression within

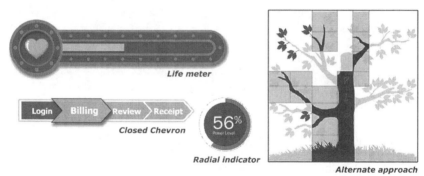

FIGURE 6.7 Progress bars are used to indicate player advancement. These images illustrate common examples of the device.

a task. In electronic or online games, progress bars are generally integrated into the interface. (See the alternative progress indicator in Figure 6.7.) But live events can use these as well; actors or game-masters often provide this information verbally to ARG teams with phrases like "You're halfway there" or "Team Alpha just checked-in with clue #3." Dashboards, on the other hand, are normally a detailed snapshot of multiple data points contained in one view for simplicity. This is very common in ARGs that use the web or mobile apps to keep players up to date. (See the example in Figure 6.8.)

Both tools promote motivation via competition because they provide players with a means of comparing their progress with that of others. Even when this information is not made public, the constant visual reminder helps to push many players forward. They also address elements 1 and 2 of Csikszentmihalyi's list.

Although competition is a great motivator for most players, we have to keep in mind that many players find active competition a de-motivator. Some players shy away from competition because of a fear of failure, past gaming experiences, or the aggressive play style of other participants. To assist these players, we often utilize methods that anonymize player identities or create multiple ways to display achievements (see multiple leaderboards and ranks mentioned earlier).

Social Connections

While a website is helpful for managing player and story activities, it is just one component of a game's digital footprint. Sending clues, story details, instructions, puzzles, and the occasional red herring via social media

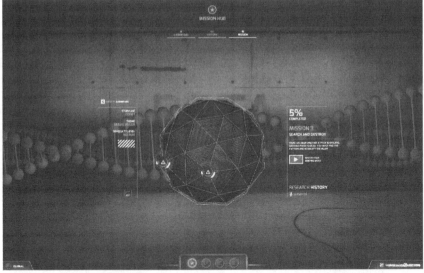

FIGURE 6.8 Dashboard from *The Black Watchmen* is heavily influenced from the game's spy theme.

apps will keep the players engaged and up to date on the game's status. Setting up Twitter, Facebook, Google+, and email accounts for NPCs are important parts of bringing the game alive. These tools can be used to facilitate two-way communication with the players, increasing tension and advancing the story without direct human intervention. (See the example in Figure 6.9.)

Beat		Details	Activity	Type	Method	Technology Options	
2	Start of Part 2	Player receives web link (video message) from Lilie Scott.	Watch video	P	tweet and url	Twitter, web host	Na ves
2.1	Player discovers combination to safe	Combination is the last four digits of the customer support phone line. Player can retrieve code from company website (About>Contact)	Find information	A	website content	web host	gr to q
2.2	Player uses combination to open safe	Acquired combination is sent via text or entered into game dashboard. If successful "secret formula" is added to player inventory	Enter information	A	webform and text chat	web host, SMS service	tris le
2.3	Player returns to Dr. Tovel's Lab with formula	Player returns to Lab to deliver formula.	Move to physical location	A	micro-location, or GPS	iBeacon with web host connection	In
2.4	Player learns of double-cross	Carl the front desk manager overheard and recorded portions of the mysterious conversation.	Ask questions	A	simulated text chat, or CCTV video	SMS service, YouTube video	co

FIGURE 6.9 Expanded beat sheet showing engagement methods and technology platforms.

This aspect of gameplay is so important that a few companies have begun developing platforms to manage this aspect of storytelling. These turnkey solutions bring together social media tools and communication services into one package that can reduce many technical and resource-heavy hurdles of building and maintaining multiple social media presences. One tool we've been investigating is Conducttr, the platform used to manage the Blink Mining example presented in Chapter 3. You can find out more about Conducttr at http://bit.ly/3_Conducttr, but here is a brief list of its key features:

- Collaborative authoring environment

- Integrated beat sheet, with scripted interactions (see Figure 6.10)

- Visual activity dashboard and timeline

- Ability to manage NPC interactions with players via social media, email, and SMS

- Templates, tutorials, and videos to get up and running

The Conducttr site contains quite a few demos that illustrate the power of the toolset. Give Faktion (http://bit.ly/6_Faktion) a try to see how video, SMS, and phone calls can be integrated in a short experience.

Whichever technology you choose to manage player activities—either paper and pencil or an online system—keep a few key factors in mind:

- Plan, test, and plan again. The beat sheet is a great way to outline required activities and identify story components. But before you start implementing those ideas, take some time to test your assumptions. Consider creating paper prototypes of various activities to see if they play out as you expected. Visit this excerpt on UX prototyping from Lynda.com for some quick tips on how to create and test prototypes—http://bit.ly/6_UX. The main goal of this activity is to identify hidden problems or complications with specific design elements before the team transitions in asset production.

- Spend a lot of time with your system and get to know it inside and out. You'll then be able to understand its strengths and weaknesses and can utilize them in your game. For example, paper is a cheap and simple way to distribute information, but it may be tough to get to all players and it is not very durable.

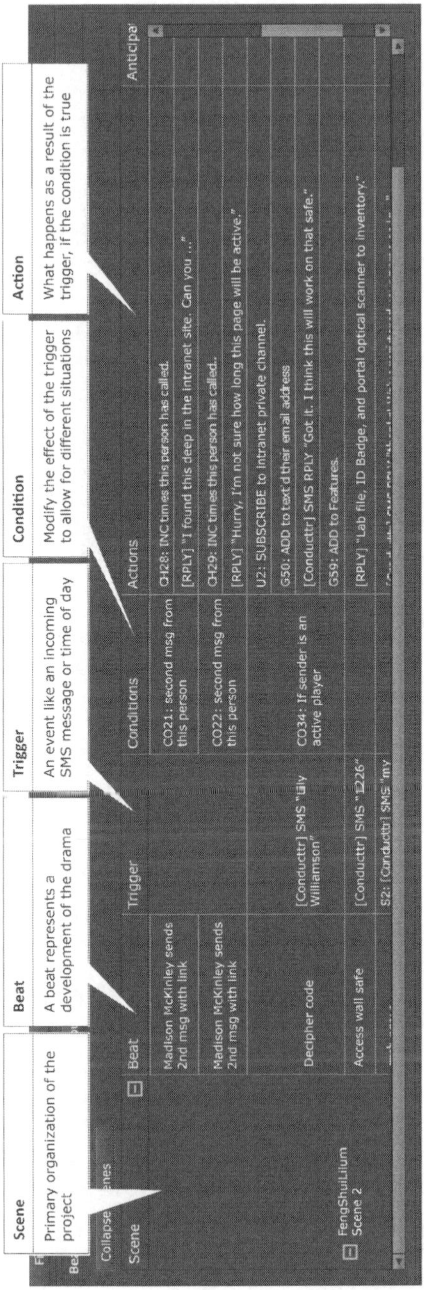

FIGURE 6.10 Beat sheet implementation in Conducttr.

- Your solution should fit into the player's experience, causing the least amount of friction. Complicated installs, lengthy downloads, and a buggy website may frustrate your audience, resulting in a negative experience for everyone involved.

ENDNOTES

[1] Csíkszentmihályi, M. (1996). *Creativity: Flow and the Psychology of Discovery and Invention.* New York: Harper/Collins (pp. 107–126)

[2] Flow represents a mental state of operation in which a person is fully immersed in the performance of an activity—http://bit.ly/6_Flow

[3] Alternate Reality Game puzzle design—http://bit.ly/6_puzzles

[4] Journey into cryptography—http://bit.ly/6_Crypto

[5] Content management systems—http://bit.ly/6_CMS

[6] Pigpen cipher font—http://bit.ly/6_Pigpen

CHAPTER 7

Dinosaur or Perfect Bird Perch

The Beast (2001) is credited as the first modern-day ARG.[1] But, ARGs for noncommercial use surfaced in the mid-1990s and the ARG concept has been explored in short stories, books, television, and movies since the early 20th century. A 1905 short story, "The Tremendous Adventures of Major Brown," hints at the ARG concept.[2] *The Game* is a 1997 movie starring Michael Douglas and Sean Penn where Douglas plays a wealthy investment banker who is given a Consumer Recreation Services game voucher by his brother (Penn) for his birthday.[3] Douglas's character is skeptical but decides to investigate the company and the game. He's pulled in to gameplay by a variety of strange events but doesn't realize he's playing. The lines between his life and the game continue to blur, resulting in conflict, danger, a rooftop leap, and ultimately self-realization.

With many years of ARG history behind us, what can we predict for the future of ARGs? Are ARGs like dinosaurs, destined for extinction in today's digital age dominated by short bursts of succinct interaction? Or are ARGs like the *Babiana ringens*,[4] evolving for functionality and adapting for the needs of different users? Mainstream learning and development industry publications like those from the eLearning Guild and the Association for Talent Development (ATD) published a number of articles on ARGs in the late part of the last decade and the early part of this one. Since then, the coverage of ARGs has been abandoned by the industry media for a focus on digital gamification through badges, leaderboards, and other game-based behavior modification techniques. The uniqueness of each ARG and the resulting difficulty in generally describing an ARG experience, the absorption of ARGs by the general gamification lexicon, and the lack of enterprise tools for ARGs have all contributed to the reduction in specific ARG exposure by the training and development media. But, ARGs are alive and well. Some recent media coverage from technology and game-based learning publications includes the following:

"Millions of People Around You Are Playing an Alternate Reality Game You Can't See," Tech.Mic[5]

"Secret Agent Students: How to Bring an Alternate Reality Game to Your Classroom," edSurge[6]

"Welcome to 'Endgame,' Google's Worldwide Augmented Reality Game That Begins Today," The Verge[7]

"Alternate Reality Games: How Can We Use Them?" Institute for Art, Science, and Technology[8]

"One Of The Most Elaborate Alternate Reality Games Ever Is Launching In 2015," readwrite[9]

The *Babiana ringens* is a South African flowering plant that has evolved a stem that can be used as a "perch," making it easier for pollinating birds to dip their beaks into its flowers. The perch varies in length depending on the region in which the flower grows to accommodate the size of birds and their beaks in that particular region.

Ingress[5] is an ARG run by Niantic Labs, a Google startup. It's a worldwide ARG where participants are divided up into two factions, the Enlightenment and the Resistance. Portals, tied to real-world physical locations in cities throughout the world, are captured for and defended by each faction. Players move around their city to collect keys, weapons, and upgrades as they capture and defend portals. Participants play through a free Android or iPhone app, which has been downloaded more than 11 million times over two years. There are over 1 million active players. It's a social game whose aim is to go beyond the directions in Google Maps and encourage residents of a city to really get to know the nooks and crannies of the places in which they live, work, and visit, along with getting to know some of the people they inhabit the cities with.

Access links to download *Ingress* from the Google Play or the Apple App Store at http://bit.ly/7_Ingress

---

The Black Watchmen[10] is being touted as "The First Permanent Alternate Reality Game." The goal of the game design is to bring the massively multiplayer online role-playing game[11] (**MMORPG**) experience to the real world, where players work together to accomplish goals as well as build their own individual player identities and specializations. Missions range from single-player to large-scale raids of thousands of players. Players can play in real-time, rewind mode, or fast-forward. The variety of play speeds allows a larger volume of players to participate by increasing the likelihood that players can fit the ARG gameplay around work, family, and daily life. *The Black Watchmen* was in alpha in 2014. Early access and the beta release were available until mid-July 2015 and the full release is now available. *The Black Watchmen* game costs $35 per season to play and is accessible online from Steam.

Access *The Black Watchmen* ARG at http://bit.ly/3_TBW

Both *Ingress* and *The Black Watchmen* represent new directions in ARGs on several fronts:

1. The ARGs are created by transmedia companies whose sole purpose is to create and run the ARG. They are dedicated, formalized groups of game designers and puppet-masters with a business plan, versus the ad hoc groups who normally work together on short-term ARG projects. The ARG is the business.

2. ARGs use custom-built emerging technologies for immersive learning. Activity in *Ingress* is driven by an ***augmented reality*** app that creates an overlay of digital information on to a virtual map of their local area. *The Black Watchmen* connects to a virtual world gameplay space built in Unity 3D. ARGs have always been transmedia

experiences, but the technology experience has mainly been fueled by static websites for information, form-based websites for entering codes, or social media tools. *Ingress* and *The Black Watchmen* both integrate advanced technologies as part of the gameplay. *The Black Watchmen* takes the technology experience to a new level by integrating the story and the gameplay across multiple levels of technology experiences (websites, virtual 3D spaces, augmented reality, etc.).

3. Just like massive open online courses (***MOOCs***), *Ingress* and *The Black Watchmen* engage thousands of players from throughout the world in a collaborative and competitive endeavor. The MOOC scalability and "business model" applied to alternate reality games is a concept that could have wide-arching impact for the ARG movement, including ARGs for business, training, and performance improvement. And, just like MOOCs, large-scale ARGs produce a massive amount of data that can be analyzed to determine best practices for ARG creation, providing insight into how players engage with ARGs for optimum experience or outcomes.

4. Both *Ingress* and *The Black Watchmen* are persistent ARGs. While there have been other persistent ARGs in the past (e.g., *World Without Oil*), the evolving story, gameplay, and collaboration between players that these games, especially *The Black Watchmen*, bring is unprecedented. The games are not only persistent but ever evolving. Persistent ARGs are like television series that you get emotionally attached to: the story, the characters, the plot twists. Traditionally ARGs have been more like movies: short-term experiences that are invigorating and immersive, but only for a short period of time.

5. *The Black Watchmen* ARG was originally financed through crowdfunding and will presumably be made sustainable through the nominal $35 per player entry fee, per season. Each season lasts three months. Up to this point ARGs have always been *free*, because they have been used for product promotion or have been internal organizational tools for training or increased engagement. The independent, pay-to-play, persistent ARG opens up a number of opportunities for monetization. There are player entry fees, but there could also be corporate sponsorship, product placement, and merchandising opportunities when the player community gets large

enough. Like many MMORPG game spaces, these ARGs could also feature a player marketplace where players buy and sell items or affordances that allow special skills or unlock advanced experiences in the game. Some game communities, like *The World of Warcraft*, have digital marketplaces with values greater than that of the GDP of some small countries.[12]

The World of Warcraft[13] is a MMORPG with over 7.1 million paid subscribers that was first introduced in 2004 and is now in its fifth expansion.

MOBILE AND WEARABLE DEVICES

Mobile devices are having an impact on all areas of communication, entertainment, and training. That same impact is being realized in ARGs. *Ingress* and *The Black Watchmen* both rely heavily on mobile devices for gameplay. The two games also require the location-based interactions that GPS-enabled mobile devices allow. The location-based gameplay in *Ingress* and *The Black Watchmen* is mobile-integrated. In a mobile-integrated game the mobile-device interactions are part of gameplay and require the player to be at a specific location to scan the code (via QR code or GPS) or find the clue through the augmented reality viewfinder. The information obtained through the mobile device interaction is then brought into the larger gameplay (which could be on a mobile device, but could also be on any other computing platform). Mobile-generated gameplay requires the player to be on the move to access or interact with content. The player's pace, trajectory, or sequence of movements can impact the information that's presented to him through the mobile device or even his status in the overall gameplay. *Zombies, Run!*[14] is an example of a mobile game that requires movement to play. The role-based gameplay challenges players to turn their evening jog into a dash for survival. Players on the run plug in their headphones to get a spike in adrenaline and added entertainment as they run from the moans and groans of zombies in the role of Runner 5, collecting supplies and running missions for settlements in a world infested with zombies. Mobile-generated gameplay, like that in *Zombies, Run!*, is more feasible for ARGs as a result of the mobile device evolution and revolution. Wearable devices like Apple Watch, Fitbit, and Lumo Lift will expand the possibilities of mobile-generated gameplay for ARGs. User-generated content as a part of gameplay is also more feasible with the now ubiquitous access to devices with cameras and audio-recording capabilities. Players can now be creators of the story as well as consumers by providing video or audio clues (false or otherwise) for other players or by using content generated from their mobile device to expand upon the content available in the ARG.

The Lumo Lift[15] is a body-positioning detector that vibrates to remind you to adjust your posture when you're not standing or sitting properly.

HEAD-MOUNTED DEVICES

Mobile devices aren't the only way to experience augmented reality. Similar to wearable devices like Apple Watch, Fitbit, and Lumo Lift that can extend experiences beyond the standard mobile device, heads-up displays (HUDs) and neural headsets create additional opportunities to take the ARG experience to another level. Google Glass is probably the most widely known heads-up display device for augmented reality. Glass users wear specially crafted eyeglass frames fitted with a Bluetooth-enabled optical head-mounted display. (See Figure 7.1.) Voice commands and multi-touch gestures control the menu selections and actions, all viewable in the heads-up display.

The Emotiv EPOC[16] is a neural headset that can be used to turn brain waves into on-screen actions, based on the user's thoughts and feelings. (See Figure 7.2.) The headset has 16 electrodes that pick up signals from your brain and translate them into actions in compatible computer

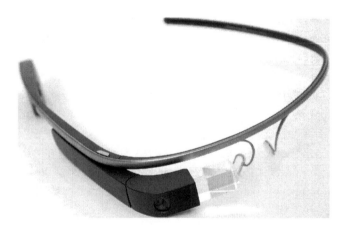

FIGURE 7.1   Google Glass.

FIGURE 7.2 Emotive EPOC.

programs. The NeuroSky neural headset[17] is another option for brain-wave input. It measures the individual's attention and meditation levels. A graduate student in the Learning Technologies Master of Science (LTMS) program at Harrisburg University created a rehabilitative game prototype that measured the user's attention and meditation through the NeuroSky neural headset. The level of attention and meditation, depending on which was required at any point in the game, controlled the avatar's movements in the game prototype. Heads-up displays and neural headsets present additional media options, expanding the transmedia world of ARGs.

GAMIFICATION

Gamification is taking business and performance improvement by storm. Since 2010 over 350 companies have launched major gamification projects.[18] By the tail end of this decade, it's estimated that the economic impact of the global gamification market will reach $5.5 billion.[19] Gamification is the application of game design techniques and mechanics to non-game experiences. As highlighted in the preface and in Chapter 1, ARGs are a form of gamification. While almost any non-entertainment game experience is now called "gamification" (even multiple-choice checks for understanding in online learning are referred to as gamification by some), true gamification is when the game-influenced experience is integrated into the daily work/life of the participant. They may not even realize they are in a gamified experience. Sound familiar? As the design of truly gamified experiences is refined and the outcomes continue to produce impact, ARGs will become an option for the larger operational strategy of the organization as well as used more in performance improvement and training activities. One game element that is often missing in the gamification experience is story. As you read in Chapter 5, story can play an important role in us emotionally connecting to an experience and more likely result in long-term memory of that experience. As was detailed throughout Chapter 5, story is an essential element of ARGs. The design, development, and integration of story in ARGs is likely to influence the evolution of gamification. Currently most gamified experiences lack a heavy story element. It's just not as necessary at this stage in gamification's evolution as are the game mechanics and feedback mechanisms. In fact, story can get in the way of brand gamification in some instances.[20] As gamification grows and evolves, there will certainly be a place for narrative and the ARG format presents a model for integrating narrative into live, subversive, and immersive gameplay.

Digital badges are leading the way as a mechanism for gamifying formal and informal education. Since 2011, about 300,000 badges have been issued using an open-sourced software developed by Mozilla (openbadges.org).[21] The badge movement is attempting to put a value on learning experiences that may or may not happen in a traditional, formal educational setting. It's a way to show that you have experience, and perhaps expertise, in a skill for which you may not have a traditional degree or certificate. Disenfranchised employers, who have increasingly found that the traditional degree is not an indication of skills or work readiness, are looking at badges as a way to identify the true skillset of job seekers. As digital badges become a more common way of signifying competencies, ARGs will be unique and fun ways for those looking for informal educational experiences to earn badges that signify the skills and worth that they can bring to employers. You might earn your team leadership and negotiation badges by navigating your ARG team through five (5) increasingly complex negotiation scenarios (the tribe of hipsters is the most difficult to negotiate with).

The multiplayer classroom is a form of gamification/ARG hybrid that is having an impact in college and K-12 classrooms. The multiplayer classroom is an instructional strategy crafted by Lee Sheldon, a game design professor at Indiana University at the time, which turns the course into a game. In a multiplayer classroom all the students start the course (game) with 0 points and level up to a desired avatar level associated with a grade for the course. They level up by completing quests, crafting items, collaborating in guilds, and challenging each other in individual and guild battles. It's *World of Warcraft* for the classroom! Students are empowered to choose their own path through various assignment types and format options in a multiplayer classroom. Experience points (XP) are earned for each activity, based on the quality of the student's performance. Teachers (game-masters) can choose to give as many options for earning XP as they would like, all within gameplay that students can engage with as much or as little as they prefer or need to—remembering that they need to level up to beat the game. The format creates opportunities for individualized pathways to learning, autonomy, collaboration, and increased motivation in the classroom. Like gamification, the multiplayer classroom format can evolve and mature by integrating elements of ARGs, especially story. As the ARG format itself evolves and adapts through integration with gamification and the multiplayer classroom, ARGs will become a more common education, training, and performance improvement strategy.

View a webinar on the multiplayer classroom facilitated for EdWeb.net in May 2014 at http://bit.ly/7_MultiplayerClassroom

---

BLENDED GAMES

Blended and hybrid learning has transformed education and training at all levels. Learning is no longer a one time event that takes place in one specific location or one specific format. There are a variety of experiences and options in blended and hybrid learning formats that allow learners flexibility in time, location, and learning preferences. As serious games mature to become more common and impactful in education and training, blended or hybrid games will become a format for consideration. ARGs have already been described throughout this book as "blended-like" and "hybrid-like" experiences. A blended game strategy may have more definitive lines between each game experience. Learners may start with a mini-game played in the browser that results in identifying competencies that need additional development. They might then begin working on the less-developed competencies in a custom-tailored, gamified online learning environment with short tutorials, videos, and community support. Then, when they return to their desk one day after lunch, they find a note on their desk that invites them to attend a meeting in the conference room. There's no indication of the topic of the meeting or why they are invited. And, the ARG begins! This type of blended game experience may take place over weeks, months, or years depending on the skills and competencies being targeted. Like blended learning, the blended game varieties and combinations are only limited by the instructional designer's imagination. And, as blended learning is just becoming "learning," so will blended learning games just become "learning."

ARG TECHNOLOGY

There are growing numbers of technology options available for serious game, augmented reality, gamification, and multiplayer classroom platforms. As you read in Chapter 6, Conducttr is an immersive story-telling and gaming platform for creating transmedia experiences. But, that's about it for ARG-specific platforms. Most ARGs are cobbled together with websites, content management systems, public social media, and custom databases. As projects like *Ingress* and *The Black Watchmen* mature and gamification evolves to include elements of ARGs, there will be more ARG-specific platforms that morph out of serious game, augmented reality, gamification, and multiplayer classroom platforms.

CONCLUSION

We really don't know what the future of ARGs is, but what you've read in this chapter is a summary of our best guesses based on observations of converging forces in serious games, gamification, employee engagement, work/life integration, technology advancements, educational pedagogy, and instructional technology. ARGs are alive and well and will be for some time. Only time will tell whether ARGs become a mainstay of organizational learning, change management, and performance improvement activities. An ARG that impacts a large technology organization to the tune of millions of dollars of increased productivity would also help spread the word about the impact of ARGs for business. Satya Nadella, give us a call.

ENDNOTES

[1] *The Beast* was the first true Alternate Reality Game—http://bit.ly/7_TheBeast
[2] History of ARGs—http://bit.ly/7_HistoryofARGs
[3] 1997 film *The Game*—http://bit.ly/7_CRS
[4] Modern evolution and adaption—http://bit.ly/7_Evolution
[5] Synopsis of the game *Ingress*—http://bit.ly/7_Ingress
[6] Bringing ARGs to your classroom—http://bit.ly/7_ARGclassroom
[7] Endgame, Google's worldwide ARG—http://bit.ly/7_Endgame
[8] Waag Society: How can we use ARGs?—http://bit.ly/7_UsingARGS
[9] Readwrite article on *The Black Watchmen*—http://bit.ly/7_readwrite

[10] Press kit for *The Black Watchmen*—http://bit.ly/3_TBW

[11] Interviews: An Experience for Everyone, Even You—http://bit.ly/7_MMORPG

[12] Virtual World Millionaires—http://bit.ly/7_GettingRich

[13] *World of Warcraft* (WoW)—http://bit.ly/7_WoW

[14] *Zombies, Run* now free—http://bit.ly/7_FreeZombies

[15] Health and fitness wearables—http://bit.ly/7_Wearables

[16] How the Emotiv EPOC works—http://bit.ly/7_Emotiv

[17] ECG & EEG biosensors—http://bit.ly/7_Biosensors

[18] 8 Surprising gamification statistics—http://bit.ly/7_GameStats

[19] What is Gamification—http://bit.ly/0_Gamification

[20] How important is story in gamification?—http://bit.ly/7_Story

[21] What can we learn from the badging movement?—http://bit.ly/7_Badges

CHAPTER 8

The Search for One-Eyed Willy

Like any adventure, your journey through the world of ARGs for learning and performance must come to an end. Or must it? We may bring you a sequel, but for now it's up to you to continue the journey on your own. You can choose to swallow the red pill or the blue pill. You may want to just continue studying the ARG concept, you may want to integrate elements of ARGs into your training and performance improvement projects, or you may want to launch a full-blown ARG experience for your next sales meeting. If you swallow the red pill, there are a number of resources for you to continue your journey beyond this book.

THE BOOK WEBSITE

The accompanying website contains live links to many of the resources in this book and we'll continue adding more as we come across them; see Figure 8.1. The site will also provide ways to build a community of "ARGs for business" enthusiasts and practitioners. Watch where you step on the website, though. There may be a rabbit hole or two. And, you don't want to twist an ankle while surfing the web!

THE BOOK RESOURCES

We'll be posting live links to the resources from throughout the book on the website. But, here's a categorized compilation for you to enjoy now.

FIGURE 8.1   What is this?

ARG Conferences

ARGFest-o-Con

   http://www.argfestocon.com/

North American Simulation and Gaming Association Conference

   http://www.nasaga.org/page/our-conferences

The CUNY Games Festival

   https://gamesfest2015.commons.gc.cuny.edu/

ARG Game Sites

Spring Revival: Camden Springs Web Site

   http://www.campdensprings.com/

The Black Watchmen

   http://www.blackwatchmen.com/

I Love Trees: Gameplay Site

   http://caelt5.harrisburgu.edu/ilovetrees/

World Without Oil

   http://worldwithoutoil.org/

Who Is Mr. Robot?

   http://www.whoismrrobot.com/

Ingress

   https://www.ingress.com/

Models

Cogs of the Cognitive Processes

   http://www.schrockguide.net/bloomin-apps.html

Flow

   https://en.wikipedia.org/wiki/Flow_(psychology)

Presentations

I Love Trees ARG Debrief

http://www.slideshare.net/apetroski/i-love-trees-arg-debrief-v3

Alternate Reality Games for Enterprise Education: Bridging the Reality Gap between Simulation and Authentic Experience

http://www.slideshare.net/pompeysie/alternate-reality-games-for-enterprise-education-bridging-the-reality-gap-between-simulation-and-authentic-experience

Make an Alternate Reality Game!

http://www.slideshare.net/nettrice/make-an-alternate-reality-game-10190076?next_slideshow=2

Transmedia Storytelling and Alternate Reality Games

http://www.slideshare.net/remotedevice/transmedia-storytelling-and-alternate-reality-games

Production Resources and Examples

ARGology

http://bit.ly/4_ARGDesign

Campaign timeline of the *Year Zero* alternate reality game

http://bit.ly/4_YearZero

Robots Are Eating the Building Rabbit Hole Video

https://www.youtube.com/watch?v=MxB8tbOTnHM

The Hero's Journey Outline

http://bit.ly/5_Hero

Brainstormer 2.0

http://bit.ly/5_Brainstorm1

http://bit.ly/5_Brainstorm2

Alternate Reality Game Puzzle Design

http://bit.ly/6_puzzles

Cipher Tools

http://bit.ly/6_Cipher

BabelStone Fonts

http://bit.ly/6_Pigpen

Conductrr: Pervasive Entertainment Platform

http://www.tstoryteller.com/

Conductrr: Faktion Demo

http://bit.ly/6_Fakition

Twine is an open-source tool for prototyping interactive, nonlinear stories

http://bit.ly/4_Twine

UX prototyping tutorial: Paper prototyping techniques

https://www.youtube.com/watch?v=FS00UIo12Xk

Publications

Finding the Future: Inside NYPL's All-Night Scavenger Hunt
   http://lj.libraryjournal.com/2011/07/managing-libraries/finding-the-future-inside-nypls-all-night-scavenger-hunt-cover-story/#_
Immersive Learning: Designing for Authentic Practice
   https://www.td.org/Publications/Books/Immersive-Learning
Spring Revival: Alternate Reality Game Breathes New Life into Old Course
   http://www.learningsolutionsmag.com/articles/617/spring-revival-alternate-reality-game-breathes-new-life-into-old-course-
Designing an Educational Alternate Reality Game
   http://bit.ly/1_ARGDesign
SILS Students, Faculty, Staff, Alumni and Friends Teamed Up for Award-Winning
   ShBANGE Project
   http://bit.ly/2_ShBANGE
Crisis Simulation: Blink Mining
   http://bit.ly/3_BlinkMining
The Threshold: Redefining Teamwork
   http://nomimes.com/threshold
The *A.I. Web Game*
   http://www.seanstewart.org/beast/intro/
World Without Oil: The Post-Game Press Release
   http://bit.ly/3_WWO
Game Development Essentials: An Introduction
   http://www.amazon.com/Game-Development-Essentials-An-Introduction/dp/1111307652
Millions of People Around You Are Playing an Alternate Reality Game You Can't See
   http://bit.ly/7_Ingress
Secret Agent Students: How to Bring an Alternate Reality Game to Your Classroom
   http://bit.ly/7_ARGclassroom
Welcome to "Endgame," Google's Worldwide Augmented Reality Game That
   Begins Today
   http://bit.ly/7_Endgame
Alternate Reality Games: How Can We Use Them?
   http://bit.ly/7_UsingARGS
One of the Most Elaborate Alternate Reality Games Ever Is Launching in 2015
   http://bit.ly/7_readwrite

ARG Resource Sites

Alternate Reality Gaming Network
   http://www.argn.com/
ARGology
   http://bit.ly/4_ARGDesign

References

FOREWORD

http://www2.deloitte.com/content/dam/Deloitte/us/Documents/technology/
us-cons-tech-trends-2012.pdf

http://engagementalliance.org/what-is-gamification/

CHAPTER 1

http://www.academia.edu/258188/Designing_An_Educational_Alternate_
Reality_Game

http://www.schrockguide.net/bloomin-apps.html

http://www.schrockguide.net/bloomin-apps.html

CHAPTER 2

http://www.bridgecapitalsolutionscorp.com/employee-recruiting-costs-versus-
employee-retention/

http://www.gallup.com/services/178514/state-american-workplace.aspx

https://www.vocoli.com/blog/may-2014/20-shocking-hr-statistics/

http://www.amazon.com/The-Hidden-Resons-Employees-Leave/dp/0814408516

http://www.mckpeople.com/au/SiteMedia/w3svc161/Uploads/Documents/
760af459-93b3-43c7-b52a-2a74e984c1aO.pdf

http://www.dalecarnegie.com/assets/1/7/Building_a_Culture-_The_Importance_
of_Senior_Leadership.pdf

http://www.haygroup.com/downloads/us/engaged_performance_120401.pdf

http://www.gartner.com/newsroom/id/1844115

http://www.campdensprings.com/

https://www.td.org/Publications/Books/Immersive-Learning

http://sils.unc.edu/news/2011/shbange

http://bit.ly/2_LearningTransfer

http://www.yukaichou.com/gamification-examples/farmville-game-mechanics-
winning-addicting/#.VR6rYuET8Rk

CHAPTER 3

http://www.argn.com/

http://www.slideshare.net/apetroski/i-love-trees-arg-debrief-v3

http://www.conducttr.com/
http://www.universityaffairs.ca/features/feature-article/playing-games-school/
http://aliceandsmith.com/
http://www.blackwatchmen.com/press-kit/
http://www.seanstewart.org/beast/intro/
http://www.argn.com/2011/09/six_to_start_gets_you_in_shape_for_zombie_
apocalypse_with_zombies_run/
http://www.argn.com/2007/07/world_without_oil_the_post-game_press_release/

CHAPTER 4

http://bit.ly/4_YearZero
http://bit.ly/4_ARGDesign

CHAPTER 5

http://bit.ly/5_Bartle

CHAPTER 6

http://bit.ly/6_Flow
http://bit.ly/6_puzzles
http://bit.ly/6_Crypto
http://bit.ly/6_Cipher
http://bit.ly/6_Pigpen
http://bit.ly/3_Steam
http://www.argn.com/
http://www.universityaffairs.ca/features/feature-article/playing-games-school/
http://www.conducttr.com/success-stories/crisis-simulation-blink-mining/
http://bit.ly/6_Threshold
http://bit.ly/3_TheBeast
http://bit.ly/3_ZombieRun
http://bit.ly/3_WWO

CHAPTER 7

http://bit.ly/7_MultiplayerClassroom
http://bit.ly/7_TheBeast
http://bit.ly/7_ARGhistory
http://bit.ly/7_CRS
http://bit.ly/7_Evolution
http://bit.ly/7_Ingress
http://bit.ly/7_ARGclassroom
http://bit.ly/7_Endgame
http://bit.ly/7_UsingARGS
http://bit.ly/7_readwrite
http://bit.ly/7_MMORPG
http://bit.ly/7_GettingRich

http://bit.ly/7_WoW
http://bit.ly/7_FreeZombies
http://bit.ly/7_Wearables
http://bit.ly/7_Emotiv
http://bit.ly/7_Biosensors
http://bit.ly/7_GameStats
http://bit.ly/0_Gamification
http://bit.ly/7_Story
http://bit.ly/7_Badges

Glossary

Achievers: One of Bartle's four player types. In general, achievers are competitive collectors, they enjoying collecting things like points, badges, items, and levels when they can be used to improve their game status. Devices like badges, titles, achievements, and focused leaderboards are good tools to highlight achiever activities.

active learning: The design of learning experiences where learners are actively engaged in the learning process through cognitive analysis, synthesis, or creation, versus being passive consumers of information as learners.

alternate reality game: An alternate reality game is a transmedia storytelling device that blurs the lines between the real world and the game world. Players can use a variety of methods to interact within both worlds while exploring the narrative, interacting with characters, and solving challenges.

augmented reality: Augmented reality (AR) is a live direct or indirect view of the physical world mediated by a computer, tablet, mobile phone, or smart device.

Bartle Test: A well-established player psychology model used to classify players in multiuser online games. See achievers, explorers, killers, and socializers.

beat sheet: A method for sequencing or outlining the ARG story.

cheat codes: Often activated by entering secret phrases or by pressing a specific sequence of controller buttons, cheat codes are special functions designers use for game testing.

constructivist: Constructivism is a theory—based on observation and scientific study—about how people learn. It proposes that people construct their own understanding and knowledge of the world, through individual experiences and reflecting on those experiences.

cryptography: The practice and study of securing messages for communication. This field of study generally manifests itself through the use of encrypting messages into puzzle form.

design document: The design document is a highly descriptive living document that organizes a project's development efforts. Created by the development team, it is the result of the collaboration between designers, artists, storytellers, and programmers as a guiding vision throughout the development process.

Easter egg: A hidden message or inside joke contained within movies or games.

eLearning: ELearning is the use of technological tools in learning. It is normally an individual experience that occurs over a short period of time (an hour or two). The eLearning experience is predefined and provides little opportunity for adjusting the design or experience based on learner interaction and feedback, until version two.

encoding systems: A system used to process and/or transmit encoded messages.

Explorers: One of Bartle's four player types. Explorers like to play the game within the game. They like to find hidden treasures, alternate pathways, Easter eggs, and unknown glitches. Variety is important to explorers. It's the reward for exploring and finding something new or unique that drives their gameplay.

game balance: The concept and the practice of tuning a game's rules, usually with the goal of preventing any of its component systems from being ineffective or otherwise undesirable when compared to their peers. Fairness, difficulty, and pacing are a few areas where game balance is used to improve the player's experience. In ARGs, this activity is also done live by puppet-masters.

game marketplace: An online store where players can buy, sell, auction, or barter items that enhance their ability to enjoy and/or win the game in some way (special powers, avatar gear, etc.). A game marketplace may also have branded items for sale that show players' fandom for the game to the world outside the game (T-shirts, mugs, pens, etc.).

game-master: Game-masters serve as referees and facilitators during the game. They often direct and assist players with questions both online and face-to-face. They are on the stage where puppet-masters are behind the scenes.

game mechanics: The methods used to design player interactions. Some typical game mechanics are actions, chance, objects, rules, skills, and space.

game objectives: In an ARG for learning, the game objectives are actually learning objectives in that they are the expected goals of the experience. They are the specific knowledge, skills, attitudes, or behaviors players should be able to exhibit following gameplay.

gameplay: Gameplay is the manner in which players interact with the game. It is the pattern of play defined by the game's rules, player-to-player collaboration, methods for overcoming challenges, and interaction with story elements.

gamification: Gamification is the application of game thinking and game mechanics to nongame contexts to promote behavior change. "Gamification's main purposes are to engage, teach, entertain, and measure to improve players' contributions and participation" (Wikipedia).

geocache, geocaching: Geocaching is a recreational activity, where participants use a Global Positioning System (GPS) or mobile device to hide and seek containers, called *geocaches* or *caches*. In ARGs they tend to be used in conjunction with puzzles, ciphers, or scavenger hunts.

go live: The data and time when the ARG is available to the public. This can be when the Rabbit Hole event is deployed or when the game is announced to a targeted audience.

hard fun: Fun doesn't mean easy. Hard fun refers to the concept that we learn best when we are challenged and engaged in focused activities.

hero's journey (or monomyth): The monomyth, or hero's journey, is a complex narrative pattern that has been established as the primary way in which stories have been structured from mythology to modern-day movies. It's a concept identified in 1949 by Joseph Campbell that illustrates a common pattern in narrative fiction: "A hero ventures forth from the world of common day into a region of supernatural wonder: fabulous forces are there encountered and a decisive victory is won: the hero comes back from this mysterious adventure with the power to bestow boons on his fellow man." Campbell's work shaped the *Star Wars* films.

Killers: One of Bartle's four player types. Killers thrive on competition and prefer player-to-player challenges, versus collaboration in gameplay. This player type likes to have an impact on the game environment via construction or deconstruction. Killers also like to control gameplay either through dominating other players via the game mechanics, the socialsphere of the game, or the game marketplace.

LARPing: A live action role-playing game (LARP) is a form of role-playing game where the participants act out their characters' actions in a fictional setting.

MD5: A cryptographic hash function that is widely used to encrypt text data.

micro-blogging: A type of blog where users make short posts and updates; think of Twitter posts and Facebook status updates.

Mihaly Csikszentmihalyi: Noted for his work in the study of happiness and creativity, Mr. Csikszentmihalyi is a distinguished professor of psychology and management at Claremont Graduate University and the former head of the department of psychology at the University of Chicago.

mini-games: Mini-games are short game experiences that take place in a larger game experience. In ARGs, mini-games are usually short challenges or distractions conducted through a separate game device. An example would be an ARG that embeds a *Pong*-like game on its website requiring the player to reach a particular score.

MMORPG: MMORPG stands for massively multiplayer online role-playing game. They are persistent online game worlds that host game play for thousands of concurrent players. The sword-and-magic fantasy game *World of Warcraft* is the most popular MMORPG with over 10 million subscribers as of November 2014. The 2011 release of *Star Wars: The Old Republic* was listed as the fastest-growing MMORPG when it hit 1 million subscribers within the first three days of its release.

MOOCs: Massive online open courses (MOOCs) were first introduced in 2008 as an offshoot of distance learning. They are aimed at providing unlimited participation and access to thousands of students using online videos, readings, problem sets, interactive forums, and social media platforms.

multimodal: Provide story elements and engagement via multiple forms of activities. The multimodal experience creates variety, which can enhance learner attention and motivation, as well as present opportunities to meet the learning preferences of all participants.

non-player character: Any game character not controlled by an active player.

PHP: PHP is a general-purpose scripting language used to develop server-side applications and services. It is used to create dynamic content or images on websites.

player characters: In traditional video games, this is the character that the player is portraying—for example, Laura Croft, Luke Skywalker, Nathan Drake, or Batman. Players rarely portray roles of this type in ARGs because they mostly play as "themselves."

puppet-master: Puppet-masters manage the ARG. Most often they are a member of the design team, but this is not always the case. During the ARG experience, the puppet-masters are often making dynamic changes to the game's progress based on player interactions. They secretly work behind the scenes while the game-masters are interacting with the players.

QR Code: A Quick Response Code (QR Code) is a type of machine-readable matrix barcode. Special applications on camera-equipped smart phones and mobile devices can be used to decode the "hidden" message.

rabbit hole: A rabbit hole marks the first contact a player might have with the game world. They are typically websites or print media that are used to draw players into the game.

red herring: A misleading or distracting clue.

scope: Scope identification is part of the project planning phase. It involves determining and documenting a list of specific project goals, deliverables, tasks, costs, and deadlines. Keeping the ARG "in scope" would mean sticking to those agreed-upon goals, deliverables, tasks, costs, and deadlines.

serious games: Serious games are simulations of real-world events, issues, or processes designed for the player to practice problem solving in the game. Although serious games can be entertaining, their main purpose is to train or educate their users.

slow-scan television: Slow-scan television (SSTV) is a picture transmission method used to transmit and receive static pictures via radio or broadcast systems. In ARGs they are used as another form of encryption for secreted messages.

SMS: Short Message Service (SMS) is a text messaging service component of phone, web, or mobile communication systems.

social learning: Formal or informal interactions enabled for the purposes of knowledge management, skill development, improved performance, or collaboration. Social learning can be analog or digital.

Socializer: One of Bartle's four player types. Socializers like to interact with other players or characters. Rather than achieving a win-state, collecting, or exploring, socializers play games for the relationships that result from gameplay.

socialsphere: The collection of often interconnected social networking sites and applications where a global conversation is ongoing.

soft launch: This term refers to the unofficial launch of your ARG. It's often used as a dress rehearsal for the live event, and it is the final opportunity to present the game to a test audience and generate a final list of tweaks. The term *soft launch* has it's roots in web development, while it's sister term *soft opening* comes from the theatre.

tangential skills: Peripheral skills that are not directly related to the achievement of a task or objective, but indirectly support success. Tangential skills are often transferable to a variety of situations and environments.

transmedia storytelling: Transmedia storytelling is the technique of a story experience across multiple platforms and formats including, but not limited to, games, books, events, cinema, and television.

twist (plot twist): An unexpected change in the story trajectory. It is a common practice used to keep the audience's attention, usually surprising them with a revelation.

Index

A

Achievements, 56–57, 82
Achiever player type, 56–57, 58
Active participation, 71, 72, 75–76
"After Action Report," 51–52
A.I. Web Game, 37
Ally characters, 64
Alpha test, 47–48
Alternate reality games (ARGs), xii
    about, 2–3
    business applications, 12–14, 15–25
    characteristics of, 6–9
    employee engagement and, 13, 15–17
    examples of, 3–5
    future of, 89–90, 98
    as gamification, 9, 95–97
    large-scale, 92
    learning connection, 9–12
    participation in, 22–25, 69–88
    persistent, 92
    production process, 39–52
    profiles of, 27–37
    scenarios, 17
    story for, 53–67
    technology, 98
    uses of, 1–2
Alternate Reality Gaming Network, 27
Analysis, Design, Development,
        Implementation, and Evaluation
        (ADDIE) process, 39, 52
Audience participation, 22–23, 69–88
Augmented reality, 91–92, 94–95

B

Babiana ringens, 89, 90
Backstory, 66

Badges, 82
Bait-and-switch, 24–25
Bartle Test of Gamer Psychology, 55, 57, 58
The Beast, 89
Beat sheets, 70–71, 73, 85, 86, 87
The Black Watchmen, 35, 77–78, 85, 91–93, 98
Blended games, 97–98
Blended learning, 19–20, 97–98
Blink Mining, 32
Bloom's taxonomy, 10–12
Brainstormer app, 64
Buddy system, 24
Business applications, 12–14, 15–25

C

Challenges, 78, 80
Character builder tools, 64
Characters
    creating, 62–64
    non-player, 3, 63, 69
    types, 62–64
Cheat codes, 56
Ciphers, 75, 81
Collaboration, 17, 19, 39
Collaborative learning, 18
Collaborative storytelling, 66
Competition, 82–84
Components, building of, 48
Computer games, 6–7
Conducttr, 86, 87, 98
Constructivist approach, to learning, 3, 9–10
Content management system (CMS), 76,
        81–82
Contextual ranking, 83
Cosmic Voyage Enterprises, 71
Creative process, 78–79
Crowdfunding, 92

Crowdsourcing, 22
Cryptography, 81
Csíkszentmihályi, Mihály, 78–79, 80

D

Dark Knight, 74–75
Dashboards, 83–84, 85
Debriefing phase, 51–52
Deep Sleep Initiative, 43–44
Design document, 43, 45–46
Development process. *see* production
        process
Digital badges, 96
Digital content, 74–76

E

Easter eggs, 56
eLearning, 6, 13
Elma Wood's Species Discovery, 5
Emotiv EPOC, 94–95
Employee engagement, 13, 15–17
Encoding systems, 80–81
Experience
        characteristics of enjoyable, 79
        designing the, 44–45
        monitoring the, 50
        player, 45–46
Experience points, 97
Explorer player type, 57, 58

F

"Fail early" philosophy, 48
Faktion, 86
Farmville, 24
Fictional story perspective, 61
Find the Future, 4, 19, 23, 65, 77
Flow concept, 79–80

G

The Game, 89
Game
        ending the, 51
        monitoring experience of, 50
        starting the, 49–50

Game balance, 61
Game-masters, 50
Game mechanics, 9
Gamification, xi, xii, 9, 95–97
Geocaching, 7
Goals, 12, 42–43
Go-live phase, 49–51
Go-live dates, 43
Google Glass, 94
Group communication, 82
Guardian characters, 64

H

Hard fun, 2
Head-mounted devices, 94–95
Heads-up displays (HUDs), 94
Herald characters, 64
Hero character, 62
Hero's journey, 59–60
Hybrid learning, 97–98

I

I Love Trees, 4, 60, 71
Images, 74
Immersion, 16, 18, 72, 76–78, 91–92
Ingress, 90–91, 92, 98
Initiation phase, 41–42
Innovation, 13–14, 18, 21–22

K

Killer player type, 55–56, 58

L

Leaderboards, 57, 82–83
Learning
        blended, 19–20, 97–98
        collaborative, 18
        constructivist approach to, 3, 9–10
        eLearning, 6, 13
        hybrid, 97–98
        social, 3, 8–9
        through ARGs, 9–12, 22
Learning mechanisms, xii

Learning objectives, 12
Live action role-playing (LARPing), 8

M

Marketplace, 55
Massive open online courses (MOOCs),
 92
McGonigal, Jane, 4, 72
Media plan, 46
Mentor character, 63
Micro-blogging, 74
Micro-challenges, 80
Mobile devices, 93–94
Monetization, 92–93
Monomyth, 59–60
Mr. Robot, 76
Multimedia storytelling, 66
Multimodal environment, 10
Multiplayer classrooms, 96–97

N

Narrative, 53–67
Neural headsets, 94–95
NeuroSky, 95
New York Public Library, 4, 19, 23
Non-player characters, 3, 63, 69

O

Objectives, 42–43, 45
Online learning, 13

P

Pacing, 75
Participation, 69–88
 active, 71, 72, 75–76
 identifying technologies based on,
  73–78
 immersive, 72, 76–78
 increasing, 22–25
 levels of, 72
 passive, 71, 72, 74–75
 planning for, 70–71
 player activities and, 71–73
 technology distractions and, 69

Passive participation, 71, 72, 74–75
Performance improvement, xii, 12
Physical space, 64–65
Plans, 40, 46, 70–71
Platforms, 81–82
Player activities, 71–73, 75
Player characters, 62–64
Player experience, 45–46
Player interactions, 70–72, 78–88
Player types, 55–58
Plot, 60–62
The Pocket, 47–48, 76
Postproduction phase, 49
Powerful learning practices (PLPs),
 30–31
Preliminary schedule, 42–44
Preproduction phase, 42–46
Print materials, 74
Problem identification, 48
Problem solving, 78
Production process, 39–52
 debriefing phase, 51–52
 go-live phase, 49–51
 initiation phase, 41–42
 milestones, 40
 planning and, 40
 postproduction phase, 49
 preproduction phase, 42–46
 production phase, 46–48
Production schedule, 42–45, 46
Productivity tools, 48
Progress bars, 82, 83–84
Prototyping, 47–48, 86
Puppet-master, 6, 50
Puzzles, 75, 79–81

Q

QR (quick response) code, 19
Que Syrah Syrah, 4, 23

R

Rabbit holes, 18, 24, 65
Rankings, 83
Realism, 2, 22
Realistic story perspective, 61
Relationships, 56

Requirements, documentation of, 42
Resources, 101–104
Robots Are Eating the Building, 53–54, 60, 65

S

Scavenger hunts, 7–8
Schedule, for production, 42–44, 46
Schrock's gears, 12
Scope, 39
Scoreboards, 57
Serious games, 6–7, 9
Setting, 11, 60–62
Shadow character, 62–63
ShBANGE, 20–21
Skill development, 17, 20–21
Slow-scan television, 75
Social connections, 84–88
Social interaction, 3
Socializer player type, 56, 58
Social learning, 3, 8–9
Social media, 3, 84–88
Socialsphere, 55
Soft launch, 49–51
Software development life cycle (SDLC),
    39, 52
Spring Fling, 18, 23
Spring Revival, 5
Story, 45, 53–67
    backstory, 66
    characters, 62–64
    collaborative storytelling, 66
    creation, 60–67
    gameplay and, 67
    perspectives, 61
    physical space and, 64–65
    player types and, 55–58
    plot, setting, and subject, 60–62
    purpose of, 53–55
    rabbit hole for, 65
    role of, 96
    simplicity vs. complexity in, 66–67
    structure, 59–60
    telling, across mediums, 66
    timeline, 65
    twists, 61
Subject, 60–62

T

Tangential skills, 3
Teams
    building, 42
    preproduction, 43
Teamwork, 17, 19, 39
Technology distractions, 69
Technology platforms, 69–71, 73–78, 86–88,
    91–92, 98
Television programs, 76
The Threshold, 36
Timeline, 65
Training, xii, 12–14, 17, 19–20
Transmedia, 9
Transmedia storytelling, 66
Treatments, 47–48
"The Tremendous Adventures of Major
    Brown," 89
Trickster characters, 64
Twists, in story, 61

U

User-generated content, 93–94

V

Videos, 74

W

Walkthrough learners, 25
Warwick Business School, 16, 18, 23
Wearable devices, 93–94
Web platforms, 81
Websites, 74, 75–76, 84
The World of Warcraft, 93
World Without Oil, 37, 72, 77

Y

Year Zero, 51

Z

Zombie, Run! 37, 93